RUNNING OUT OF END TIMES

PREPARING THE CHURCH WHILE THERE'S STILL TIME

ISRAEL AND CARRIE HERNANDEZ

DEDICATION

This book is dedicated to our Father who created us, to our Lord and Savior, Jesus Christ who came and died for us, and to our Holy Spirit who helps us to live a life that pleases Him each and every day.
Thank you God!

CONTENTS

RUNNING OUT OF ENDTIMES

This book may be the second most important book you will ever read. The most important book you will ever read is the Bible. All the information in this book is from the Word of God, and not from crazy "revelations". As we wrote it, God gave us insight into His Word. Insight that showed us connections between many verses throughout the Bible with the events in Revelation. Some may ask, why write a book about something that is already in the Bible? Well... two main reasons. First, the events in the End Time are all over the Bible, not just in a book or a chapter. Second, and most important, most Christians don't read the Bible.

The importance of this book is to know what time we are living in, knowing the events that have to happen and how to prepare for them. Many will be deceived by false prophets, preachers, and those ignorant of the End Times scriptures and the coming antichrist government. Also this book is written for those who will be left behind, the lukewarm, the worldly Christians and the unbelievers. I highly recommend (and encourage) you to put a copy of this book in the hands of an unbeliever so he or she can come to Christ when these events start to occur.

I invite you to read and pray about what you are reading. Not with a set mind, but with a mind that is open to allowing God to show you what the Bible says. On many topics in this book I was wrong for years because I learned and believed what preachers were saying. Please try to forget all the previous opinions you have heard in preachings or read in your study Bibles and examine each verse with fresh eyes. So let's take the denominational glasses off and let the Holy Spirit guide us.

I want to add, that as we worked on this book and studied the Bible over and over again, we have found that the book of Revelation isn't full of symbolism. It contains spiritual truths, codes that can be decoded from the same Bible, and also events that will really happen that we don't yet understand.

How this book started

In the spring of 2014 I had just moved to the Downriver area in the state of Michigan, just 10 minutes from the city of Detroit. I started to assist at a church that had great fellowship. But God called me to separate myself from the fellowship and to spend more time seeking Him. Eventually God forced me to step out of the church to teach me and to prepare me for this book.

Right after leaving that church, I was doing nothing but working my full time job, praying and watching preaching on T.V. My hunger for God was increasing day by day. One day I noticed that for the past week every preacher I had watched was talking about the End Times. Even in an app from a ministry I was listening to, the theme was End Times. Then the next week was the same. Everything I watched happened to be about End Times. I realized that God was talking to me and telling me to start studying the End Times.

During that time I watched a preacher talking about the Rapture. He said that the Rapture will be in the middle of the Tribulation. I said to myself "this guy is wrong, the church will be Raptured before the Tribulation". Then the following week I watched another preacher saying the same thing. That time God told me in my heart, "study the Bible on the End Times events". And so I did.

I spent around a year spending time studying the Bible on many events of the End Times. It was fascinating how my eyes were opened to the scriptures. This time I left behind everything that I knew and prayed to the Holy Spirit, "please, help me understand." And He did. I spent all those days without listening to other opinions. I just focused on the Bible and let the Holy Spirit teach me.

As I'm writing this, the year is 2021 and I have learned much more on this topic. Especially while studying about the End Times with my wife (sometimes even arguing). Even so, she has been a great help to me.

I pray that the Holy Spirit guides you through this book as He guided me in my study.

The condition of the Church to be Raptured

Now may the God of peace Himself sanctify you completely; and may your whole spirit, soul, and body be preserved blameless at the coming of our Lord Jesus Christ.
I Thessalonians 5:23 NKJV

The condition of Christianity today is probably the worst that it has ever been. The Church is so lukewarm and dead that it is frustrating for those whose lives are dedicated to the Lord. We have so many false doctrines accepted in the Church that many people think are biblical. My heart has been crying out to the Lord to bring revival, because I think that that's the only way the Church will wake up.

Jesus is coming back for His Church very soon, but not for today's Church. I've heard a lot of preachers saying over and over that Christians are sinners, we can't stop sinning, and that we are all hypocrites. Guess what! Jesus isn't coming for a sinning hypocritical Church! But He is coming back for a Bride: holy, spotless, without wrinkles, without blemishes and faultless! So if you are a hypocrite, repent! If you sin every day, I'm sorry to say but it is because you are in the flesh every day.

I, in my best estimate, believe that if Jesus comes this Sunday for His Church, next Sunday most churches will be as full as normal. There is no fire in most churches, there is no passion and there is no holiness!

Pursue peace with all people, and holiness, without which no one will see the Lord: Hebrews 12:14 NKJV

We have lost the first love and we need to repent and do the first works as the Lord Jesus said in the book of Revelation. We need to start a revival in our hearts, in our own family, and then in our churches and communities. Let's be the ones who lead in the time of troubles that are ahead of us. The Church will be purified by fire during tribulations and trials. Revival is not a biblical promise, but a great falling away is. Even so, we can pray to God to send revival around the world. We need revival!

Revive us again Lord! It's my prayer. Do it again!

The Rapture

The Rapture of the Church is an event that is clear in the Bible. The Church will be caught up, or snatched away, from this earth to be with the Lord in heaven. The phrase "caught up" means taken by force. The great majority of Christians believe in the Rapture, even though there are disagreements on when it will take place. It is important to know that not understanding if the Rapture will be before, in the middle or after the Tribulation doesn't mean that you are not saved. But having this doctrine wrong can be catastrophic to the church.

Is the Rapture biblical?

For this we say to you by the word of the Lord, that we who are alive and remain until the coming of the Lord will by no means precede those who are asleep. For the Lord Himself will descend from heaven with a shout, with the voice of an archangel, and with the trumpet of God. And the dead in Christ will rise first. Then we who are alive and remain shall be caught up together with them in the clouds to meet the Lord in the air. And thus we shall always be with the Lord.

Therefore comfort one another with these words.
I Thessalonians 4:15-18 NKJV

This is a clear verse that proves the Rapture of the Church and how it will happen. The Lord Himself, meaning Jesus, will descend for His Bride with a shout. He shouts not to call us, but to order the angels to gather us to Him, as He says in Matthew 24.

And He will send His angels with a great sound of a trumpet, and they will gather together His elect from the four winds, from one end of heaven to the other.
Matthew 24:31 NKJV

Now the ones who are dead in Christ will rise first and we will meet them in the clouds with the Lord. We don't know how long will pass between the dead rising and when we are caught up, but they will be first. Every "real" born again Christian on the earth will be Raptured next and we won't die. Our bodies will be transformed but we won't experience death.

Will all the children be Raptured?

This is a common question, or concern, when we talk about the Rapture. How about children? Will they be Raptured? And the answer is not explicitly in the Bible but we can assume that the children of the Christians will be Raptured with the Church. I'm talking about children under the age of accountability, whatever age that may be. And the verse that I will use for this situation makes a distinction between a child with at least one believing parent and the one with no believing parents.

For the unbelieving husband is sanctified by the wife, and the unbelieving wife is sanctified by the husband; otherwise your children would be unclean, but now they are holy.
I Corinthians 7:14 NKJV

Again, this doesn't mean that only the Christians' children will be Raptured, but I believe for sure children with at least one believing parent will. I know there are some who believe all children will be

Raptured but we don't know that. And someone may say "God won't let children suffer", well… Many children are suffering now so we can't use that logic. And if God will Rapture all children then no child should be born after the Rapture. We don't know and it is better to say that we don't know than to say something we can't prove.

Private Rapture

This is something that I have heard many times, the private Rapture. The problem with this is that it isn't biblical. We read in Matthew 24:31 when the Rapture will take place and before that, this will happen;

Then the sign of the Son of Man will appear in heaven, and then all the tribes of the earth will mourn, and they will see the Son of Man coming on the clouds of heaven with power and great glory.
Matthew 24:30 NKJV

This isn't the second coming when Jesus will establish His kingdom on earth but the Rapture of the Church. When Jesus returns to the Earth He will be riding on a white horse (Revelation 19:11) not on the clouds. So there's no private Rapture but all eyes will see Him and all who are left behind will mourn.

Behold, He is coming with clouds, and every eye will see Him, even they who pierced Him. And all the tribes of the earth will mourn because of Him. Even so, Amen.
Revelation 1:7 NKJV

Can we predict the day of the Rapture?

It is impossible for anyone to know when the Rapture will take place. Every single person that has tried to predict the Rapture of the church or the End of the World has failed miserably. Some people "predict" these events to take money from people and then they are gone. Others have dreams about the Rapture and the Tribulation and think that God gave them a date for the Rapture or a 'window' of time. Since 2014 every September 21st or 23rd the Rapture will happen according to some youtubers. A lot of them give you a bunch of Bible verses taken out of context and many people believe. I guess they don't know their Bible.

"But of that day and hour no one knows, not even the angels of heaven, but My Father only. But as the days of Noah were, so also will the coming of the Son of Man be.
Matthew 24:36-37 NKJV

When Jesus said "no one knows" and "but My Father only" that is exactly what He meant. "No one" in the original Greek means "no one". Therefore no human knows and will never know when the Rapture will take place. The season yes, but the year, month and day not even the angels know. Mark 13:32 says that not even the Son knows the day or the hour. But it is so easy to fall into that nonsense when we don't read the Bible.

Is the Rapture imminent?

The idea that the Rapture is imminent is simply that Jesus can Rapture the church at any moment and nothing has to happen before that. The issue is not if He can do it, but if He will. The only way to know is to study the Bible. But I'll tell you ahead that the imminent Rapture of the church is not Biblical. There are many things that have to happen before the Rapture occurs, and remember to keep your denominational glasses off.

One of the Bible verses that people use to support the belief that the Rapture is imminent is Matthew 24:24-44

Watch therefore, for you do not know what hour your Lord is coming. Therefore you also be ready, for the Son of Man is coming at an hour you do not expect.
Matthew 24:42, 44 NKJV

Of course you have to take it out of context to make it support the imminent Rapture idea. These scriptures say that we don't know the hour of the Rapture. It doesn't say "I will come back at any moment". There is no verse in the Bible that says that it can happen at any moment. This imminent Rapture doctrine is tied with the Pre-Tribulation Rapture, so when we get to that part of this book you will see more clearly that both of those doctrines lack Biblical support. Instead they are based on opinions and supported by taking verses out of context.

Another verse that is very often used to support the belief in imminent Rapture is in 1 Thessalonians 5:1-3

But concerning the times and the seasons, brethren, you have no need that I should write to you. For you yourselves know perfectly that the day of the Lord so comes as a thief in the night. For when they say, "Peace and safety!" then sudden destruction comes upon them, as labor pains upon a pregnant woman. And they shall not escape.
I Thessalonians 5:1-3 NKJV

"As a thief in the night" that has to mean that it will take everyone by surprise, right? No. He's talking about those who will say "Peace and safety!" Before you think I'm taking it out of context let's read the next verse.

But you, brethren, are not in darkness, so that this Day should overtake you as a thief. You are all sons of light and sons of the day. We are not of the night nor of darkness.
I Thessalonians 5:4-5 NKJV

The Day won't come as a thief in the night for those who are not in darkness but are in the light of the Lord. God will warn us before all this takes place. Not so that we can get right with God, so we don't get left behind, since we should be ready all the time, because we don't know if we will be in the Rapture or in the "dead in Christ" group. That's what I think every time I see a post on social media that says "Christ is coming! Get ready Church!" Let me tell you something about that, if you need a sign to be ready then you are not the Church. Get ready now because you don't know if you will make it till tomorrow. The signs showing that the end is near should encourage us to keep working harder to reach the lost and bring them to the feet of Jesus.

Another thing most people ignore about the phrase "coming as a thief" is that even during the last part of the wrath of God on the earth, Jesus still says "I'm coming as a thief."

"Behold, I am coming as a thief. Blessed is he who watches, and keeps his garments, lest he walk naked and they see his shame."
Revelation 16:15 NKJV

That's when the sixth Bowl of the Wrath of God is poured. So we know that that phrase is not referring to an imminent Rapture nor a Pre-tribulation Rapture.

Preterism view

Now, brethren, concerning the coming of our Lord Jesus Christ and our gathering together to Him, we ask you, not to be soon shaken in mind or troubled, either by spirit or by word or by letter, as if from us, as though the day of Christ had come.
II Thessalonians 2:1-2 NKJV

I'll continue this chapter by addressing the doctrine that teaches that all the End Times events have already happened. In the time of the apostle Paul there were some people who believed that the second coming already happened. I know about some prominent preachers who believe the very same thing that Paul warned them not to believe. The only way to know if the End Times already happened is using the Bible and history. Very easy. At the same time it will be very clear that the Rapture is not imminent. But of course we need to be sure that the scripture that we use to support a preterist view was totally fulfilled (God doesn't kind of fulfill His Word... He fulfills it completely and accurately.)

The abomination that causes desolation

"Therefore when you see the 'abomination of desolation,' spoken of by Daniel the prophet, standing in the holy place" (whoever reads, let him understand),
Matthew 24:15 NKJV

This is an event that some people believed already happened because of the desecration of the temple in 168BC. The Greek king Antiochus IV erected a statue of Zeus in the temple and sacrificed a pig on the altar. The problem with that is Jesus himself said "when you see", talking about the future. The other argument is that the temple was destroyed in 70AD so it happened then. Well, no. The temple was destroyed but there wasn't an abomination placed inside it. Let's see what Paul wrote about it.

Now, brethren, concerning the coming of our Lord Jesus Christ and our gathering together to Him, we ask you, not to be soon shaken in mind or troubled, either by spirit or by word or by letter, as if from us, as though the day of Christ had come. Let no one deceive you by any means; for that Day will not come unless the falling away comes first, and the man of sin is revealed, the son of perdition, who opposes and exalts himself above all that is called God or that is worshiped, so that he sits as God in the temple of God, showing himself that he is God.
II Thessalonians 2:1-4 NKJV

So according to the apostle Paul, the gathering of the saints won't happen until that man of sin, the anti-Christ, sits in the Temple declaring himself God. That hasn't happened yet so the Rapture is not imminent.

Another example from the End Times that needs to happen before the second coming is the mark of the Beast. I won't get into what is the mark of the beast in this chapter but the Bible in the book of Revelation says...

He causes all, both small and great, rich and poor, free and slave, to receive a mark on their right hand or on their foreheads, and that no one may buy or sell except one who has the mark or the name of the beast, or the number of his name.
Revelation 13:16-17 NKJV

There is no time in history that the whole world, or most of it, was forced to have a mark in the forehead or right hand to buy or sell. I heard a pastor argue that during the holocaust, all Jews were forced to tattoo a number on their hands to buy or sell. Now this is when history comes into play. The only Jews who were forced to have a number tattooed on their arms where the ones in the Auschwitz concentration camp. And also the tattoo with the numbers was done on the left arm. Not on the right hand or forehead.

Now that we have it very clear that the End Times is a future occurrence of events, we can move to the subject that brings more disagreement in the church: When will the Rapture take place? There are three different beliefs in the timing of the Rapture, Pre-Tribulation, Mid-Tribulation, and Post-Tribulation. I want to first point out that even when there is disagreement with the timing of the Rapture we don't have to let that divide us as the Church. I have seen many times how people in the church attack other Christians verbally, insulting them, calling names and even putting in doubt their salvation just because they believe in a different timing for the Rapture. Those who don't have the bible on their side to back their belief seem to get especially upset and defend their point by attacking other Christians. This is pathetic and has no place in the Church of Christ. I will explain each one of the three beliefs and why those who believe in them think that their timing is the right timing. I will also explain what God has shown me as I mentioned in the introduction.

Pre-Tribulation Rapture

This doctrine holds that the Rapture will take place before the Tribulation. They believe that the Church will be raptured before the bad things start to happen. I used to believe in Pre-Tribulation Rapture or better said, I repeated what I was taught about this viewpoint. I had no idea how to defend this doctrine nor did I have a single Bible verse to support it. But after God moved me to study the End Times it became very clear to me that Pre-Tribulation is not in the Bible. When someone believes in Pre-Tribulation, I always ask for just one verse that supports that view, just one. I remember texting with an old friend from Puerto Rico about the End Times. She was like me years ago, she believed what had been taught to her and I asked her for just one Bible verse to support Pre-Tribulation. After more than two years she never gave me one verse and a teacher went to her church teaching about the Rapture. She never found the verse and now she doesn't believe in Pre-Tribulation Rapture anymore.

There is a belief that the whole Pre-Tribulation Rapture doctrine started with John Nelson Darby. Others say that it started before him, but the truth is that Darby made it popular when most people believed that the church would go to Tribulation. But again with no clear Biblical reference but stretching verses and taking them out of context. There is also a lot of "this means this or that" that is used today to support a Pre-Tribulation Rapture. They say, "because this verse says this, that it means that". Let see some of the verses that are used to support the Pre-Tribulation Rapture doctrine and see what they really say. I know some of you are putting the denominational glasses on again but you won't be able to read the scriptures with them. Please put the Word of God first, then your denomination.

God didn't appoint us to wrath

and to wait for His Son from heaven, whom He raised from the dead, even Jesus who delivers us from the wrath to come.
I Thessalonians 1:10 NKJV

For God did not appoint us to wrath, but to obtain salvation through our Lord Jesus Christ,
I Thessalonians 5:9 NKJV

This is the main argument that those who believe in the Pre-Tribulation Rapture use to support their belief but none of those verses say anything about Rapture before Tribulation. For this to support their view it would have to say "For God did not appoint us to tribulation…" Do you see how this little change makes the verse actually say what they think it says? This is where most people are confused. They don't understand that the wrath of God and the Tribulation are not the same. The Tribultion is the devil against the church, the wrath is God judging the world. To understand this better I'll explain with more details when we get into the Mid-Tribulation Rapture.

John called up

After these things I looked, and behold, a door standing open in heaven. And the first voice which I heard was like a trumpet speaking with me, saying, "Come up here, and I will show you things which must take place after this."
Revelation 4:1 NKJV

This verse is probably the one that those who believe in a Pre-Tribulation Rapture stretch the most. This verse simply means that John heard a voice like a trumpet saying, "Come up here" and telling him that he will show him things that will take place in the future. But for some people this is the Rapture! How can it be? There are two main ideas of a Pre-Tribulation Rapture that they try to take from this one verse;

      o   Come up here

Because John was called to come up, that has to be the Rapture of the church, right? No. That simply means that John was called up. He was the only one to come up and He didn't see any other Christians being caught up to heaven. If this was the Rapture, instead of going straight to heaven, John should have met the dead in Christ in the air with the other Christians. Also, the Church won't be 'called up' but we will be 'caught up'. Now as I said before, caught up means taken by force. The angels will gather us together and snatch us away.

      o   The church is not mention after this

The church is not mentioned anymore in the Book of Revelation after John is told to "come up here", which means that the church is Raptured before bad things happen, right? No, No and No. The word "church" is not mentioned again in the book of Revelation after chapter 3 but the Christians are still mentioned many times and are also called saints.

And I said to him, "Sir, you know." So he said to me, "These are the ones who come out of the great tribulation, and washed their robes and made them white in

15

the blood of the Lamb.
Revelation 7:14 NKJV

When He opened the fifth seal, I saw under the altar the souls of those who had been slain for the word of God and for the testimony which they held.
Revelation 6:9 NKJV

And the smoke of the incense, with the prayers of the saints, ascended before God from the angel's hand.
Revelation 8:4 NKJV

The Church is still mentioned by other names but it is still the same Church so this argument also doesn't make sense.

As you can see none of these verses say clearly that the Church will be Raptured before the Tribulation and this is the problem. Just like many false doctrines, the use of verses out of context is the only way to defend it.

Recently I was watching a well-known pastor talking about the Rapture (I wanted to see how he would support his position). He used to be a Post-Tribulation believer but now he is Pre-Tribulation. I was amazed by how he took every verse out of context. I told my wife that I wanted to stop watching the video because I would lose all respect for that preacher. She wanted to keep watching and soon the preacher said the most crazy stuff I have ever heard about the End Times. The Pre-Tribulation Rapture preacher turned to a Pre and Post-Tribulation Rapture guy. He said that there will be a Rapture before the Tribulation and a second Rapture at the end.

The main verses that this preacher used to explain his brand new doctrine was Luke 17 and Luke 21. I want to take some time to explain some points he made and easily refute them. Again, the only way to keep a Pre-Tribulation Rapture doctrine alive is to make up alternate interpretations from verses that have their own clear meanings.

One will be taken and another will be left

Two women will be grinding together: the one will be taken and the other left. Two men will be in the field: the one will be taken and the other left."
Luke 17:35-36 NKJV

 The argument about these verses, according to his Pre-Tribulation point of view, is that there is peace in that time because two women are grinding grain and two men in the field. He says if there is tribulation in the world, and one third of the world has been destroyed, and a star named Wormwood has fallen and destroyed most of the Earth, then nobody would be working in the field.

 Again, bad conclusion. He was comparing it to a Post-Tribulation Rapture so the argument may makes sense in that context. But the Rapture won't occur after what they call "Tribulation" but in the middle. As I said, I'll get more into that in the Mid-Tribulation Rapture chapter, but for now understand that the Tribulation will be a 3.5 years period, then the "Wrath of the Lamb" (Seven Trumpets) and the "Wrath of God' (Seven Bowls) will follow. Now, even during the 3.5 years of Wrath people need to eat, so working in the field and grinding grain will still happen in some parts of the world.

The days of Noah and Lot

And as it was in the days of Noah, so it will be also in the days of the Son of Man: They ate, they drank, they married wives, they were given in marriage, until the day that Noah entered the ark, and the flood came and destroyed them all. Likewise as it was also in the days of Lot: They ate, they drank, they bought, they sold, they planted, they built; but on the day that Lot went out of Sodom it rained fire and brimstone from heaven and destroyed them all. Even so will it be in the day when the Son of Man is revealed.
Luke 17:26-30 NKJV

 According to the preacher, these verses are the best proof of the Pre-Tribulation Rapture. "Jesus explains how the Church will escape the Tribulation as Noah escaped the flood". He continued; "Lot escaped from the destruction of Sodom and Gomorrah and the

Church will escape the destruction that is coming to the world".

Those verses don't even talk about Rapture but about the judgement that is coming to the world. Jesus isn't talking about the Church at all but about the unbelievers and sinners. They will be drinking and having fun sinning, and indulging in immoral behavior, and they won't see the destruction that will be taking place, the Wrath of God. The apostle Paul wrote about it;

For when they say, "Peace and safety!" then sudden destruction comes upon them, as labor pains upon a pregnant woman. And they shall not escape.
I Thessalonians 5:3 NKJV

This verse makes sense only if you think you have to choose between Pre and Post. There will be a sense of peace for some before the Rapture of the Church, and at the same time Christians will be persecuted. This is a good argument against a Post-tribulation viewpoint (because no one will be saying peace and safety during the trumpets and bowls during the wrath) but not for a specific Pre-Tribulation Rapture. As I already said, Jesus was talking about the lost having peace not the saints. But if you want to talk about Noah and Lot they weren't taken by force. Also, neither of them was taken to a better place, Noah ended up in a world completely destroyed and Lot was alone with his two crazy daughters.

Pray and you won't suffer

Watch therefore, and pray always that you may be counted worthy to escape all these things that will come to pass, and to stand before the Son of Man."
Luke 21:36 NKJV

The wrong interpretation of this verse is that God will give you a chance to escape from the suffering of the Tribulation if you pray and watch. It sounds good if you take it out of context, but we need to read all the verses before that one to understand. In verse 28, Jesus makes very clear when the Rapture will be near, so everything before that verse applies to the Church. War, nations against nations, great earthquakes, famines, pestilences and persecution will happen before verse 28, and still the Rapture hasn't come yet but is near. Now if you don't want to call this the Tribulation then what do you call it? Luke 21:36 is talking about escaping from the "Wrath of God" not the Tribulation.

As I said in the beginning there's not a single verse in the Bible that talks about a private imminent Pre-Tribulation Rapture. This is a false doctrine from the 1800's that the devil is using to deceive the Church so we don't prepare for what's coming. Also think about this, the condition of the Church today is very bad. We have become so worldly, so selfish, we don't love each other, in fact many Christians seem to hate each other, we are lovers of material things and lovers of money. Sexual immorality is acceptable now at all levels inside the Church. Think about it, if the Rapture of the Church occurs today, most churches will have a big crowd next Sunday. There is not a Pre-Tribulation Rapture and if ever there was going to be one, it would have been cancelled because of our carnality.

RUNNING OUT OF ENDTIMES

Post-Tribulation Rapture

The most popular Post-Tribulation Rapture view is that the Church will go through the whole 7 years of the combined Tribulation and Wrath of God; and then the Rapture will happen at the same time Jesus is returning to establish His kingdom. There are many variations of this view that place the Rapture at different points. I won't go through all of these... it will be a waste of time. Instead we'll just show why this position as a whole can't be true.

This doctrine teaches with verses that may seem to be backing their position, but they have to be twisted to make them fit. In the same way that those who believe in the Pre-Tribulation Rapture take verses out of context to support it, those who believe in a Post-Tribulation Rapture do this too.

Correcting this position is quite easy, if we just move the timing 3.5

years earlier, then the verses no longer need to be twisted, and suddenly make complete sense. Plus now we can use some verses that the Pre-Tribulation doctrine uses incorrectly. One example is the verse about wrath;

For God did not appoint us to wrath, but to obtain salvation through our Lord Jesus Christ,
I Thessalonians 5:9 NKJV

We can use this verse to refute the idea that the Church will still be here to suffer the "Wrath of God" revealed in Revelation. Those events are to judge the world and their wickedness, not the Church. I have heard the "God will protect the Church during that time" argument, but there's no scripture to back it up. The 144,000 from the tribes of Israel will be sealed and protected but there is no mention of the Church. A side note, those 144,000 are actual people not symbols of something else.

They sang as it were a new song before the throne, before the four living creatures, and the elders; and no one could learn that song except the hundred and forty-four thousand who were redeemed from the earth. These are the ones who were not defiled with women, for they are virgins. These are the ones who follow the Lamb wherever He goes. These were redeemed from among men, being firstfruits to God and to the Lamb. And in their mouth was found no deceit, for they are without fault before the throne of God.
Revelation 14:3-5 NKJV

These are actually people, not symbols of something else. The bible is specific about gender and character. If John had wanted to describe the church as a whole (a common symbolism argument) would he have been specific about the number, the tribes, the gender and the fact they had never been with women? "These are the ones who were not defiled with women, for they are virgins…Also in their mouth was found no deceit or lies." The person that comes to my mind when I think of them is someone like Daniel the prophet. Some may argue that there are not 144,000 young Christian-Jewish men in Israel, so that can't be talking about people. My answer is simple, there are around 7 million Jews in the world and the Bible doesn't say they have to live in Israel, but that they are from the tribes of Israel.

And second it will take only one Revival in Israel to have 144,000 virgin men get saved. Remember the Wales Revival when more than 100,000 people got saved in less than a few months.

The Church is also clearly not the Woman in the wilderness, as this is the remnant of Israel. If you want to see more on this go to the timeline section called the Woman Nourished.

Now coming back to the time of judgement, if the Church will go through the whole time of destruction there is a big problem. God will have to punish us the same as the world and that can't be possible.

Then out of the smoke locusts came upon the earth. And to them was given power, as the scorpions of the earth have power. They were commanded not to harm the grass of the earth, or any green thing, or any tree, but only those men who do not have the seal of God on their foreheads. And they were not given authority to kill them, but to torment them for five months. Their torment was like the torment of a scorpion when it strikes a man. In those days men will seek death and will not find it; they will desire to die, and death will flee from them.
Revelation 9:3-6 NKJV

This terrifying thing will occur at the Fifth Trumpet. All men (and women) will be tortured so badly that they will seek to die but they won't be able to do so. For five months! Again, "All men," except the ones that have been sealed (the 144,000), so everyone else will be tortured by those creatures. Just with this evidence we can disprove the Post-Tribulation Rapture doctrine, but I want to show you more so you can be 100% sure.

Also a few people believe that the Rapture will occur at the Seventh Trumpet of Revelation, if you believed that probably by now you have changed your mind about it. Or do you still think the Church will suffer the Wrath? Do you think they will still be buying and selling and giving in marriage at the Seventh Trumpet? Also the verse about the "last trump" would have been very confusing for the Christians in Corinth who received the letter, as John didn't write about the trumpets in Revelation until 20 years later.

Matthew 24 is the main source used to defend the Post-Tribulation Rapture, but again it has to be taken out of context to fit their narrative. I heard somebody who believed in a Post-Tribulation Rapture using Matthew 24:30-31 as the main proof of their position. The interpretation is that after the Tribulation, Jesus will come to establish His kingdom, we will be Raptured and join Him on the clouds, and then we will come down with Him.

Then the sign of the Son of Man will appear in heaven, and then all the tribes of the earth will mourn, and they will see the Son of Man coming on the clouds of heaven with power and great glory. And He will send His angels with a great sound of a trumpet, and they will gather together His elect from the four winds, from one end of heaven to the other.
Matthew 24:30-31 NKJV

I completely agree, this is the Rapture of the Church but this verse doesn't say anything about Jesus returning to Earth. Jesus will meet us in the clouds, He doesn't come all the way down. And neither does it say that we will return with Him at this point. We can't add an interpretation that isn't there. Nowhere in the Bible does it say that we will be Raptured and come back in the same hour. It's not until Mathew 25:31 that He actually comes back with His angels to sit on His throne and reign.

If you go to Revelation 19, the Bible mentions the marriage supper of the Lamb. It's mentioned right before the Lord's return on a white horse. I think this is why Post-Tribulation Rapture believers place the Rapture right before the Lord's return. But if you read carefully, the "great multitude" is not new people that just came from the Earth, they were there already. The marriage supper of the Lamb is the preparation for the Bride of Christ, the Church, to return with Jesus and reign with Him. And I believe that as Jesus was with the disciples for three and a half years, we the Bride, might be with Him for three and a half years. It is called The Marriage Supper of the Lamb, not a fast food dinner.

And to her it was granted to be arrayed in fine linen, clean and bright, for the fine linen is the righteous acts of the saints.
Revelation 19:8 NKJV

The Church will be arrayed in fine linen, clean and bright, and we will follow Jesus when He returns to establish His kingdom. But there's no mention of Rapture or that a new group of people has arrived as in Revelation 7:14. By the way, this verse is also used as a Post-Tribulation Rapture by some but the timing is easy to disprove.

After these things I looked, and behold, a great multitude which no one could number, of all nations, tribes, peoples, and tongues, standing before the throne and before the Lamb, clothed with white robes, with palm branches in their hands, Then one of the elders answered, saying to me, "Who are these arrayed in white robes, and where did they come from?" And I said to him, "Sir, you know." So he said to me, "These are the ones who come out of the great tribulation, and washed their robes and made them white in the blood of the Lamb. Revelation 7:9, 13-14 NKJV

The book of Revelation is mostly in chronological order, but there are chapters that give details about specific events, but not in a specific order. Now that we understand that, we need to see if this verse is in chronological order or not. The best way to know if it is, is to read the verse in context. Revelation 7 is a continuation of Revelation 6:12, The Sixth Seal. That means that there has to be a Seventh Seal. And to make this Rapture account a Post-Tribulation Rapture, the Seventh Seal has to be the Lord's return, but it isn't.

The Seventh Seal is when the Seven Trumpets are given to the angels. The Trumpets are followed by the Bowls of the Wrath of God. The Seven Trumpets judgment alone will take several years to be completed. One example is the Fifth Trumpet when the creatures will torture all men that are not part of the 144,000 sealed for five months. So it's impossible to place the Rapture at the end of the Wrath of God. We are promised tribulation in this world but told that we are not appointed to wrath. This is why the distinction between the Tribulation and the Wrath is so important. Remember this, the Tribulation is the Seven Seals, after that is the "Wrath".

To conclude this chapter let's understand a few points. There is no place in the End Times scriptures that mention the Church being protected on earth during the time of destruction and judgment to the world. Only the 144,000 from the tribes of Israel will be. God didn't appoint us to wrath, but promised us tribulation. And also, at the end, most of the world will be destroyed, most of the population is dead, so what good will it be to be raptured for no more than an hour? How is this something that we can *'comfort each other'* with?

And adding to that, according to Jesus, people will be having normal lives during the time of the Rapture of the Church, but after the Wrath of God is complete everything will be destroyed.

Likewise as it was also in the days of Lot: They ate, they drank, they bought, they sold, they planted, they built; but on the day that Lot went out of Sodom it rained fire and brimstone from heaven and destroyed them all. Even so will it be in the day when the Son of Man is revealed.
Luke 17:28-30 NKJV

The last point is that in the time of Lot, God told Abraham that he wouldn't destroy Sodom and Gomorrah if there were five righteous people. So God removed the righteous people from the land that was to be judged before the wrath was poured in it. But don't forget, Lot did face tribulation from the wicked people before leaving.

Mid-Tribulation Rapture

In this chapter I'll show why the Mid-Tribulation Rapture is the only one of the three Rapture theories that make sense. It reconciles the verses that cause conflict between the Pre and Post-Tribulation viewpoints. It isn't really in the middle of the Tribulation, but at the end. The rest of the seven years is Wrath, not Tribulation. This means that the "7 year Tribulation," or the 70th Week of Daniel, is really divided into two parts, just as Daniel describes. The first 3.5 years of tribulation happens to the Church, and the second 3.5 years of judgment and Wrath is for the sinners. So the best way to call it is "Post-Tribulation Pre-Wrath". I will give you many scriptures, that don't need a different interpretation, and can be read in their original context.

I want to start with Matthew 24, because that was where I understood that the Pre-Tribulation Rapture didn't exist.

Now as He sat on the Mount of Olives, the disciples came to Him privately, saying, "Tell us, when will these things be? And what will be the sign of Your coming, and of the end of the age?"
Matthew 24:3 NKJV

 Take in consideration that, when the Bible was written, there were no chapters or verses. So Matthew 24 and 25 are the same conversation. Many people think that when the disciples asked Jesus about when the temple will be destroyed, the signs of your coming and of the end of the age, that all the answers are in Matthew 24. First, that the disciples asked those questions doesn't mean Jesus answered them all, or that He told them everything. For example, Jesus never told them when the temple would be destroyed, even though that subject started the whole conversation in chapters 24 and 25.

Jesus told them what was relevant to them as the Church, and what they could handle at that time. What you will find in these two chapters is the signs before the Rapture, but most of these chapters are about preparing yourself for it. There is a mention of the Second Coming, which is when He returns to establish His kingdom. But what you won't find in these chapters is the Wrath of God or the judgment of the world, because the Church won't be there, even though people will still get saved during the destruction of the world.

The Rapture

Then the sign of the Son of Man will appear in heaven, and then all the tribes of the earth will mourn, and they will see the Son of Man coming on the clouds of heaven with power and great glory. And He will send His angels with a great sound of a trumpet, and they will gather together His elect from the four winds, from one end of heaven to the other.
Matthew 24:30-31 NKJV

 Let's break down these verses to understand a few points that will disprove some of the common errors regarding the Rapture. First, the idea of a private Rapture isn't possible because it clearly says that "they will see the Son of Man". Everyone will see the sign of the Son of Man and they will mourn. So no matter where you put the time of the Rapture it won't be private.

Second, Jesus coming in the clouds isn't the Second coming. In this event Jesus doesn't come down to earth, but stays in the clouds. When He comes again to establish His kingdom, He will be riding on a white horse. Also, Jesus sent His angels to gather the Church. If He is to come down next, I don't think He would miss that part in His explanation of the End Times. It isn't until Matthew 25:31 when Jesus makes reference to the Second coming, and He speaks of it as a separate event.

"When the Son of Man comes in His glory, and all the holy angels with Him, then He will sit on the throne of His glory.
Matthew 25:31 NKJV

The Tribulation

Now that we have the Rapture in Matthew 24:30-31, and we know that it isn't the same event as the Second Coming, we need to see if the Rapture will be before or after the Tribulation. The answer is easier and clearer than you'd expect. It blew my mind when I read it, and I asked myself why I missed it so many times. The key verse is no more and no less than the verse before this one, verse 29.

"Immediately after the tribulation of those days the sun will be darkened, and the moon will not give its light; the stars will fall from heaven, and the powers of the heavens will be shaken.
Matthew 24:29 NKJV

This is the clearest verse about the time of the Rapture that you'll find, *"after the tribulation of those days"*. The Rapture won't come until the Tribulation passes. Let's put all three verses together so we can understand better.

"Immediately after the tribulation of those days the sun will be darkened, and the moon will not give its light; the stars will fall from heaven, and the powers of the heavens will be shaken. Then the sign of the Son of Man will appear in heaven,

and then all the tribes of the earth will mourn, and they will see the Son of Man
coming on the clouds of heaven with power and great glory. And He will send
His angels with a great sound of a trumpet, and they will gather together His elect
from the four winds, from one end of heaven to the other.
Matthew 24:29-31 NKJV

You can't miss that. It doesn't get much clearer than that. Jesus
Himself said that we will go through the Tribulation, again not the
same as the Wrath. In most Bible versions the word "tribulation" is
used in Matthew 24:29. The NIV uses "distress" which means the
same thing, but NIV in Spanish uses "tribulación," that is clearly
tribulation. Even if you believe that the word tribulation isn't the
same in the original Greek, just put your finger on Matthew 24:31
and read everything before that until verse 4. Everything between
verses 4 and 31 is what the Church will go through. So let's see if it
looks like tribulation to you.

Matthew 24

- Verse 4 - Deceivers will come
- Verse 5 - Many false christs
- Verse 6 - Wars and rumors of wars
- Verse 7 - Nations against nations, famine, pestilences and
  earthquakes in various places
- Verse 8 - This is just the beginning
- Verse 9 - They will deliver you to tribulation, kill you and you
  will be hated by all nations
- Verse 10 - Betray one another and hate one another
- Verse 11 - False prophets will deceive many
- Verse 12 - Lawlessness will abound, love of many will grow
  cold
- Verse 13 - You must endure to be saved
- Verse 15 - The abomination that causes desolation
- Verse 16 - People in Judea must flee
- Verse 19 - Woe to those who are pregnant or nursing.
- Verse 21 - Great Tribulation such as never been before

- Verse 24 - False christs and false prophets, deceived if possible the elect
- Verse 29 - After the tribulation of those days

How does that look to you? To me it looks like Great Tribulation! Did you notice that the word tribulation was used three times in those verses? Only once was it called the Great Tribulation.

For then there will be great tribulation, such as has not been since the beginning of the world until this time, no, nor ever shall be.
Matthew 24:21 NKJV

That Great Tribulation will be for the Church and the Jews. The world will hate us so much for the name of Jesus, and today we can see how this hate is growing in our country and around the world. One of the signs that is mentioned in verse 12 of Matthew 24 is "lawlessness will abound". We can also see that this is being fulfilled today all over the United States and around the world.

Coming back to the timing of the Rapture, the events that Jesus described are for the tribulation time not the Wrath. There will be great events that will take place during the Seven Trumpets and the Bowls of the Wrath of God that aren't mentioned in Matthew 24 or 25. These events are bigger than the ones Jesus warns us about. For example, one third of the Earth is destroyed by fire, something like a mountain hits the earth, a star (meteor) falls into the ocean, 144,000 men from the tribes of Israel are sealed and protected... but why didn't He tell us of these bigger disasters? Again, Jesus mentioned what is for the Church before the Rapture, what will happen after it isn't relevant for them at that time. That's why the book of Revelation was given to the apostle John late in his life, after he was the only original apostle left.

Matthew 24 and The Seven Seals

It's very clear that the Pre-Tribulation Rapture can't be true according to Matthew 24. And now to prove that the Rapture in this

31

chapter is in the middle of the so-called "7 year tribulation" we're going to compare Matthew 24 to Revelation 6 and 7. You will be fascinated to see that both chapters are the same, almost identical.

When He opened the second seal, I heard the second living creature saying, "Come and see." Another horse, fiery red, went out. And it was granted to the one who sat on it to take peace from the earth, and that people should kill one another; and there was given to him a great sword.
Revelation 6:3-4 NKJV

For nation will rise against nation, and kingdom against kingdom...
Matthew 24:7 NKJV

When He opened the third seal, I heard the third living creature say, "Come and see." So I looked, and behold, a black horse, and he who sat on it had a pair of scales in his hand. And I heard a voice in the midst of the four living creatures saying, "A quart of wheat for a denarius, and three quarts of barley for a denarius; and do not harm the oil and the wine."
Revelation 6:5-6 NKJV

And there will be famines...
Matthew 24:7 NKJV

When He opened the fourth seal, I heard the voice of the fourth living creature saying, "Come and see." So I looked, and behold, a pale horse. And the name of him who sat on it was Death, and Hades followed with him. And power was given to them over a fourth of the earth, to kill with sword, with hunger, with death, and by the beasts of the earth.
Revelation 6:7-8 NKJV

And you will hear of wars and rumors of wars...
Matthew 24:6 NKJV

And there will be famines, pestilences...
Matthew 24:7 NKJV

When He opened the fifth seal, I saw under the altar the souls of those who had been slain for the word of God and for the testimony which they held. And they cried with a loud voice, saying, "How long, O Lord, holy and true, until You

judge and avenge our blood on those who dwell on the earth?"
Revelation 6:9-10 NKJV

"Then they will deliver you up to tribulation and kill you, and you will be hated
by all nations for My name's sake.
Matthew 24:9 NKJV

I looked when He opened the sixth seal, and behold, there was a great
earthquake; and the sun became black as sackcloth of hair, and the moon became
like blood. And the stars of heaven fell to the earth, as a fig tree drops its late figs
when it is shaken by a mighty wind.
Revelation 6:12-13 NKJV

"Immediately after the tribulation of those days the sun will be darkened, and the
moon will not give its light; the stars will fall from heaven, and the powers of the
heavens will be shaken.
Matthew 24:29 NKJV

After these things I looked, and behold, a great multitude which no one could
number, of all nations, tribes, peoples, and tongues, standing before the throne and
before the Lamb, clothed with white robes, with palm branches in their hands,
Then one of the elders answered, saying to me, "Who are these arrayed in white
robes, and where did they come from?" And I said to him, "Sir, you know." So
he said to me, "These are the ones who come out of the great tribulation, and
washed their robes and made them white in the blood of the Lamb.
Revelation 7:9, 13-14 NKJV

"Immediately after the tribulation of those days the sun will be darkened, and the
moon will not give its light; the stars will fall from heaven, and the powers of the
heavens will be shaken. Then the sign of the Son of Man will appear in heaven,
and then all the tribes of the earth will mourn, and they will see the Son of Man
coming on the clouds of heaven with power and great glory. And He will send
His angels with a great sound of a trumpet, and they will gather together His elect
from the four winds, from one end of heaven to the other.
Matthew 24:29-31 NKJV

I have found that the way to understand the book of Revelation is
understanding the rest of the Bible. I've heard many times that the
last book of the Bible is full of symbolism and can't be understood

today. That's false. The book of Revelation is written in such a way that we can decode it with the rest of the scriptures. Take the Seven Seals as an example of this. The events are in Revelation, but also in Matthew 24, Mark 13 and Luke 21. In each passage the events are all the same. So Jesus told us, and it's recorded in four places, what will be the signs of the Rapture and of His return.

 Now, we can't say Matthew 24 is talking about a Post-Tribulation Rapture because of Revelation 8

When He opened the seventh seal, there was silence in heaven for about half an hour. And I saw the seven angels who stand before God, and to them were given seven trumpets.
Revelation 8:1-2 NKJV

 The Seven Trumpets are given after the saints are taken *out of the Great Tribulation*. Like we already said, it will take 3.5 years for the judgment of the Trumpets to be completed, followed by the Seven Bowls of the Wrath of God.

Tribulation vs Wrath

And I saw in the right hand of Him who sat on the throne a scroll written inside and on the back, sealed with seven seals.
Revelation 5:1 NKJV

 We believe that the scroll contains the final judgment of God to this world. It's important to notice that there are things written on the front of the scroll and on the back. We think it is probably the judgment of the Seven Trumpets on one side and the Seven Bowls of the Wrath of God on the other side. The Seven Seals are holding the scroll closed, and every time one seal is open something that has been held by God is released. It's like God is allowing things to happen in the world, but it isn't Him directly doing these things. That's why it is important to see the difference, so we understand the meaning of Post-Tribulation Pre-Wrath.

 The Wrath is never called tribulation because it is the judgment of

God over the evil people and this cursed world. I believe the Seven Trumpets are the Wrath of the Lamb over those who persecuted, tortured and killed the Bride of Christ.

and said to the mountains and rocks, "Fall on us and hide us from the face of Him who sits on the throne and from the wrath of the Lamb! For the great day of His wrath has come, and who is able to stand?"
Revelation 6:16-17 NKJV

When you read the Seven Trumpets judgment, notice that there are angels releasing the judgments, something that you won't find in the Seven Seals. This time it isn't God allowing things, but it is Him directly sending the destruction and judgment. At this time it's impossible for the Church to still be here (some of the people left behind can still be saved but they aren't spared from the wrath because they waited too long).

And I looked, and I heard an angel flying through the midst of heaven, saying with a loud voice, "Woe, woe, woe to the inhabitants of the earth, because of the remaining blasts of the trumpet of the three angels who are about to sound!"
Revelation 8:13 NKJV

Look for a single verse in the Bible that says that the Christians will be protected from these judgements and you won't find it. Again, only the 144,000 sealed will be spared from all the sufferings, and the remnant of Israel will be protected by the two wings of a great eagle that carry her into the wilderness. Everyone left behind will have to suffer the Seven Trumpets judgment, plus persecution will still happen. Many new Christians will be decapitated when they reject the mark of the beast and refuse to worship his image.

And I saw thrones, and they sat on them, and judgment was committed to them. Then I saw the souls of those who had been beheaded for their witness to Jesus and for the word of God, who had not worshiped the beast or his image, and had not received his mark on their foreheads or on their hands. And they lived and reigned with Christ for a thousand years.
Revelation 20:4 NKJV

If you still think that the Woman who is nourished is the Church then think about this... why would God only protect some of the Christians at this time? Why are many Christians being persecuted and beheaded as they refuse to take the mark while God protects some of His people in the wilderness? How is this fair? If the woman is the Church and the Rapture hasn't happened yet then all Christians should be protected in the same way. But we know that after the woman is carried into the wilderness the dragon is enraged with the woman and goes "*to make war with her offspring, who keep the commandments of God and have the testimony of Jesus Christ. (Revelation 12:17)*."

The Bowls of the Wrath of God are delivered over the rest of humanity.

Then I heard a loud voice from the temple saying to the seven angels, "Go and pour out the bowls of the wrath of God on the earth."
Revelation 16:1 NKJV

At this point, all the Christians who were left in the world are dead, decapitated. There is no mention of people getting saved during this final judgment, but people will curse God during three of the Seven Bowls and nobody repents.

And men were scorched with great heat, and they blasphemed the name of God who has power over these plagues; and they did not repent and give Him glory. They blasphemed the God of heaven because of their pains and their sores, and did not repent of their deeds. And great hail from heaven fell upon men, each hailstone about the weight of a talent. Men blasphemed God because of the plague of the hail, since that plague was exceedingly great.
Revelation 16:9, 11, 21 NKJV

Like we already saw, it's impossible for the Church to go through these last judgments. Now some people believe the Rapture will happen before the Seven Bowls of the Wrath of God. That theory doesn't have biblical evidence, nowhere in Revelation do we see people arriving in heaven before the bowls, and likewise we don't see verses in other areas of the bible supporting this belief. The last trump cannot be referring to the seventh trumpet because by this time all Christians are dead, as are the two witnesses. How can those *who are alive and remain* be preceded by the dead in Christ if there are none left alive?

And those who dwell on the earth will rejoice over them, (the Two Witnesses) *make merry, and send gifts to one another, because these two prophets tormented those who dwell on the earth.*
Revelation 11:10

 If Christians are still dwelling on the Earth are they making merry when God's prophets are killed? Were they tormented by them during the 42 months? Christians are not dwelling on the Earth at this time. By now they were either raptured or they have been beheaded for refusing the mark.

He was granted power to give breath to the image of the beast, that the image of the beast should both speak and cause as many as would not worship the image of the beast to be killed. He causes all, both small and great, rich and poor, free and slave, to receive a mark on their right hand or on their foreheads,
Revelation 13:15-16 NKJV

If Christians are still dwelling on the earth did they worship the beast and accept the mark? No. They didn't. They died. Every last post Rapture believer dies rather than accepting the mark.

Then a third angel followed them, saying with a loud voice, "If anyone worships the beast and his image, and receives his mark on his forehead or on his hand, "he himself shall also drink of the wine of the wrath of God, which is poured out full strength into the cup of His indignation. He shall be tormented with fire and brimstone in the presence of the holy angels and in the presence of the Lamb.
"And the smoke of their torment ascends forever and ever; and they have no rest day or night, who worship the beast and his image, and whoever receives the mark of his name."
Revelation 14:9-11 NKJV

RUNNING OUT OF ENDTIMES

THE ANTICHRIST

The Antichrist will be a big player in the End Times events. We won't know who he is until we are at that moment in time when he will be revealed. And yes, we will see him.

Let no one deceive you by any means; for that Day will not come unless the falling away comes first, and the man of sin is revealed, the son of perdition,
II Thessalonians 2:3 NKJV

In this chapter, I'm going to explain to you some details about his time as a ruler, so that we can have an idea of what to look for at that time. Trying to guess who it may be today is entertaining but useless, (even though I have three candidates). The only way to know is when he, the antichrist, fulfills the Bible prophecies regarding him.

The easiest one to know is when the antichrist confirms a covenant with many (nations) for seven years. Many believe that that covenant will include a deal with Israel and Palestine that will allow the reconstruction of the Temple.

Then he shall confirm a covenant with many for one week; But in the middle of the week He shall bring an end to sacrifice and offering. And on the wing of abominations shall be one who makes desolate, Even until the consummation, which is determined, Is poured out on the desolate."
Daniel 9:27 NKJV

In the middle of the seven years he will break the covenant and stop the sacrifice and offering in the Temple. This event is probably tied with the mortal wound that the beast of Revelation will have. Now, when that wound is healed is when Satan, the dragon, gives all his power to the antichrist.

Now the beast which I saw was like a leopard, his feet were like the feet of a bear, and his mouth like the mouth of a lion. The dragon gave him his power, his throne, and great authority. And I saw one of his heads as if it had been mortally wounded, and his deadly wound was healed. And all the world marveled and followed the beast.
Revelation 13:2-3 NKJV

Many people believe that he will actually die and come back to life. But the Bible says that he is mortally wounded but was healed, so he won't die, but almost die. Now after that is when Satan gives his power to him, the antichrist will be worshiped and will demand the worship of all people on earth.

who opposes and exalts himself above all that is called God or that is worshiped, so that he sits as God in the temple of God, showing himself that he is God.
II Thessalonians 2:4 NKJV

That's when the abomination that causes desolation will occur in the Temple. We don't know for sure what will be 'set up' in the Temple that will be an abomination. We don't know, but what we know is that the antichrist will go to the Temple and will declare himself God.

The mark of the Beast

This is probably the most speculated upon topic regarding the End

Times. I won't spend too much time on this but my point will be very solid in disproving other ideas. The Bible is very clear about what the mark of the beast is.

He was granted power to give breath to the image of the beast, that the image of the beast should both speak and cause as many as would not worship the image of the beast to be killed. He causes all, both small and great, rich and poor, free and slave, to receive a mark on their right hand or on their foreheads, and that no one may buy or sell except one who has the mark or the name of the beast, or the number of his name. Here is wisdom. Let him who has understanding calculate the number of the beast, for it is the number of a man: His number is 666.
Revelation 13:15-18 NKJV

The mark of the beast won't be a microchip or an invisible tattoo. I know that most people believe in the possibility but I also know that most people don't read the Bible, especially the book of Revelation. Let's see what the scriptures say and understand.

and that no one may buy or sell except one who has the mark or the name of the beast, or the number of his name.
Revelation 13:17 NKJV

Not everyone will get the mark. There are three different types of things that will be implemented.

- The mark (probably a logo of some sort)
- The name of the beast (his human name)
- The number of his name (666?)

I put a question mark on the number 666 because of what the next verse says.

Here is wisdom. Let him who has understanding calculate the number of the beast, for it is the number of a man: His number is 666.
Revelation 13:18 NKJV

The verse says "calculate" the number of the beast and then gives us 666. It's possible that the number 666 will help us know who the antichrist is but his "number of a man" could be different.

Coming back to microchips, I believe that very soon we will have a new world currency. That will be a kind of cryptocurrency or digital currency. China is about to release their digital currency in the 2022 Winter Olympics. Everything will be digital including paychecks, bill payments, buying and selling, and pretty much all transactions that involve "money". I'm not sure how they are going to roll out their method in which people will be able to carry their digital wallet, but right now they are using cellphones for that.

It's possible that soon every human will be required to have a microchip implanted. Or at least all people in the more technologically advanced countries, but eventually it will be required around the world. The antichrist will reign over the whole world.

It was granted to him to make war with the saints and to overcome them. And authority was given him over every tribe, tongue, and nation.
Revelation 13:7 NKJV

What I believe according to the scriptures, is that when the time comes that the mark of the beast will be implemented, they will impose a deadline for everyone to get the mark. After the deadline passes, all the digital wallets of the people who haven't been marked will be shut down, so they can't buy or sell. Remember the mark is actually a mark, not a financial device.

Can I get the mark and still be saved?

This is a real question that many people have, and the only answer is in the Bible. The short answer is NO. The long answer is NO and this is why;

Then a third angel followed them, saying with a loud voice, "If anyone worships the beast and his image, and receives his mark on his forehead or on his hand, he himself shall also drink of the wine of the wrath of God, which is poured out full strength into the cup of His indignation. He shall be tormented with fire and brimstone in the presence of the holy angels and in the presence of the Lamb. And the smoke of their torment ascends forever and ever; and they have no rest day or

night, who worship the beast and his image, and whoever receives the mark of his name."
Revelation 14:9-11 NKJV

 The Bible is very clear in this. You have to decide to renounce Jesus, agree to worship the beast, and recognize him as the only true god. You won't be tricked into getting the mark. They won't hide it from the people. You won't get it by accident. You either take the mark, worship the beast and his image, or you will be beheaded. But if you decide to take the mark there is no salvation for you, or anyone who takes it.

End Times Chronology

According to all of our studies, with prayer and guidance from the Holy Spirit, we put together a timeline of the events of the last seven years. Each major event will be designated by a letter, and explained with supporting verses.

Please Note:

- Week - 7 years
- Time - 1 year
- Times - 2 years
- Half a time - ½ a year
- 3.5 years = 42 months = 1260 days = Time, times and half a time

There are some important things to understand in order for the End Times timeline to make sense. We know that there is not one like this out there and we want to explain some of what led us to this timeline.

Every verse had to make sense in relationship to all the other verses.

This led us to rewriting it until everything fit. As we worked out the conflicts we began to think that the 7 years might end before the return of Christ, but we didn't believe it until we found verse after verse supporting it. Every timeline that we compared didn't stand up to all the verses of the scriptures (including our first drafts). To be biblically accurate all the accounts and times have to fit. We will never put out a timeline if we know that there is an important piece left out because it doesn't fit our opinion. First let's list some verses that talk about three and a half years.

The clearest verses are the ones that say things will last for 1,260 days.

And I will give power to my two witnesses, and they will prophesy one thousand two hundred and sixty days, clothed in sackcloth."
Revelation 11:3 NKJV

Then the woman fled into the wilderness, where she has a place prepared by God, that they should feed her there one thousand two hundred and sixty days.
Revelation 12:6 NKJV

There are also verses that say that events will last for 42 months.

"But leave out the court which is outside the temple, and do not measure it, for it has been given to the Gentiles. And they will tread the holy city underfoot for forty-two months.
Revelation 11:2 NKJV

And he was given a mouth speaking great things and blasphemies, and he was given authority to continue for forty-two months.
Revelation 13:5 NKJV

And these verses say that things will happen for a time, times and half a time. Notice that the first event listed is also described above so we know that the belief that this is 3.5 years is correct.

He shall speak pompous words against the Most High, Shall persecute the saints of the Most High, And shall intend to change times and law. Then the saints shall be given into his hand For a time and times and half a time.

Daniel 7:25 NKJV

Then I heard the man clothed in linen, who was above the waters of the river, when he held up his right hand and his left hand to heaven, and swore by Him who lives forever, that it shall be for a time, times, and half a time; and when the power of the holy people has been completely shattered, all these things shall be finished.
Daniel 12:7 NKJV

But the woman was given two wings of a great eagle, that she might fly into the wilderness to her place, where she is nourished for a time and times and half a time, from the presence of the serpent.
Revelation 12:14 NKJV

There are also some verses that are confusing and didn't neatly fit into the timeline. We've listed them here but we will explain them as we go.

"And from the time that the daily sacrifice is taken away, and the abomination of desolation is set up, there shall be one thousand two hundred and ninety days.
Daniel 12:11 NKJV

Blessed is he who waits, and comes to the one thousand three hundred and thirty-five days.
Daniel 12:12 NKJV

Then I heard a holy one speaking; and another holy one said to that certain one who was speaking, "How long will the vision be, concerning the daily sacrifices and the transgression of desolation, the giving of both the sanctuary and the host to be trampled underfoot?" And he said to me, "For two thousand three hundred days; then the sanctuary shall be cleansed."
Daniel 8:13-14 NKJV

All of these verses have to fit together seamlessly or the timeline won't stand. The Bible always explains itself so we searched the scripture until we had a better understanding. Now we're going to show you how we arrived at this timeline.

Let's start with the concept that is the most strange and will need the most support (especially for those of you who know your Bible.)

The seven year covenant ends with the seventh trumpet. I know, it sounds weird but stay with us for a minute as we explain. It started with an argument between my wife and me, about what the middle of the seven weeks means. Does middle in Hebrew mean middle? Yes.

At this point we were trying to fit the Abomination of Desolation occurring in the middle of the week with the 1290 days until the end. If the Abomination of Desolation occurs at the actual middle of the week then it would have been 1260 days until the end. These verses confused us and sent us back to prayer and searching the scripture for wisdom.

I first found that there had to be a gap between the Abomination of Desolation and the beginning of the 42 months that the woman is protected by Eagle Wings in the Desert. This comes from Daniel 11:31-36 when he describes how after the Abomination of Desolation there will be a time when 'those with understanding' will instruct many; yet for many days they will fall by the sword and flame. **After these days** it will be given to the antichrist to prosper until the wrath has been accomplished. In Revelation 13:5 the antichrist is given authority for 42 months.

From this we know that there are 42 months from the time he starts prospering in the holy city until the end of the wrath. We know these 42 months don't happen immediately after the Abomination of Desolation because of the many days that 'those with understanding' will instruct many and be persecuted.

Now we had an issue. IF middle means middle then the 42 weeks needed to start at the Abomination of Desolation. Then there was this crazy verse that said that from the time of the Abomination of Desolation there will be 1290 days. My wife had put the Abomination of Desolation 30 days before the middle of the week and wanted very badly to defend this decision to make the 1290 days fit. I was more willing to extend the 1290 days past the seven years. She was confused by this idea. She finally stopped trying to make close to the middle good enough and started looking for verses to support my idea and this is what we found.

In Revelation 10:7 it says that *in the days of the sounding of the seventh angel, when he is about to sound, the mystery of God would be finished, as He declared to His servants the prophets.* (We believe this mystery includes the 70 weeks of Daniel. Look at what the angel says in Daniel 12:7 *'it shall be for a time, times and half a time; and when the power of the holy people has been completely shattered, all these things shall be finished.'*) Then in Revelation 11:15-19 it says that *the seventh angel sounded: and a loud voice from heaven said "The kingdoms of the world have become the kingdoms of our Lord and of His Christ, and He shall reign forever and ever....* Then later in this account, as elders are worshiping Him they say He has taken His great power and that His wrath has come.

Now if the reign and wrath of God have come at the sounding of the seventh trumpet, what do we do with all the verses that happen after that trumpet is sounded? The bowls have yet to be poured out. The sixth bowl is demonic spirits that will gather all the men of earth together to fight against God at the battle of Armageddon. These things take time to accomplish so we can't believe that the bowls are all poured out instantly.

So now we are left with a period of time after the seven years in which the bowls are poured out, and Christ returns to the earth on the white horse. This now makes the 1290 days make so much more sense. Also the 1235 days until the cleansing of the temple also makes more sense. We aren't confined to a seven year period. The seven years was a time appointed for the Jewish people. When the two witnesses die the last of the believers are gone and the 'power of the holy people is crushed'. From this point on there are no longer any people saved. All that are left have accepted the mark of the beast and all that are left are enemies of God except the 144,000 and the remnant of Israel. Now the worst of His wrath pours out as He takes up rulership of the earth.

If you have really studied Daniel you may be wondering about the 2300 days.

And he said to me, "For two thousand three hundred days; then the sanctuary

shall be cleansed."
Daniel 8:14 NKJV

This verse confuses some simply because they miss the fact that it is concerning the daily sacrifices not the stopping of them. From the time the daily sacrifices start (which cannot be pleasing to God as He was the ultimate sacrifice and the Jews can no longer offer the blood of bulls and lambs to atone for their sins) until the time the temple is cleansed is 2300 days. This now fits neatly into our timeline.

Now that the strangest aspect of our timeline is explained lets explain the rest.

The timeline is on the next page.... If you want a pdf copy please email us at outofendtimes@gmail.com or visit https://www.outofendtimes.com/

Each item on this timeline is explained in the next section. Look for the letter that is before each item and find the corresponding section for the explanation of what it is and the verses that led us to placing it where we did on the timeline. We tried to put it in an order that makes the most sense, but please feel free to look up the points that most interest you, or just read it in order.

RUNNING OUT OF ENDTIMES

Chronology

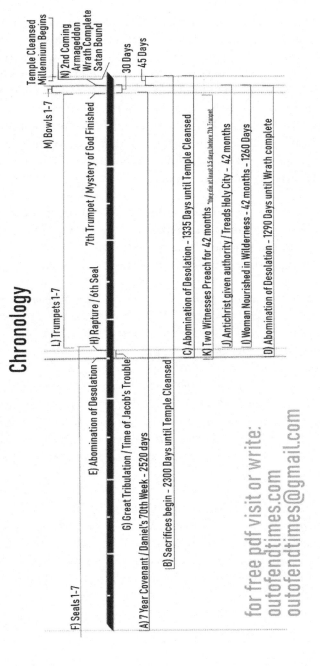

F) Seals 1-7

L) Trumpets 1-7

H) Rapture / 6th Seal

7th Trumpet / Mystery of God Finished

M) Bowls 1-7

Temple Cleansed
Millennium Begins

N) 2nd Coming
Armageddon
Wrath Complete
Satan Bound

30 Days

45 Days

E) Abomination of Desolation

G) Great Tribulation / Time of Jacob's Trouble

A) 7 Year Covenant / Daniel's 70th Week - 2520 days

B) Sacrifices begin - 2300 Days until Temple Cleansed

C) Abomination of Desolation - 1335 Days until Temple Cleansed

K) Two Witnesses Preach for 42 months *they die at least 3.5 days before 7th Trumpet

J) Antichrist given authority / Treads Holy City - 42 months

I) Woman Nourished in Wilderness - 42 months - 1260 Days

D) Abomination of Desolation - 1290 Days until Wrath complete

for free pdf visit or write:
outofendtimes.com
outofendtimes@gmail.com

51

A) Seven year covenant

Daniel 9:20-27 talks about the seventy weeks of Daniel. Daniel is told that there are seventy weeks appointed for his people. In Hebrew a week is a group of seven. Seven days, weeks, months or years could be called weeks. In this case we know from the context that it is seventy groups of seven years. The verse says that after the first sixty nine weeks the Messiah will be cut off but not for Himself. This means that He will be killed. Jesus died after the 69 weeks and the church age started. The last week that was appointed for the Jewish people is yet to be fulfilled. This is the last seven years before Christ returns to rule and reign.

In Daniel 9:27 it specifically talks about how the antichrist (the prince who is to come) will make a covenant with many for one week, but in the middle of the week he will bring an end to sacrifice and offering and cause the Abomination of Desolation.

"Know therefore and understand, That from the going forth of the command To restore and build Jerusalem Until Messiah the Prince, There shall be seven weeks and sixty-two weeks; The street shall be built again, and the wall, Even in troublesome times. And after the sixty-two weeks Messiah shall be cut off, but not for Himself; And the people of the prince who is to come Shall destroy the city and the sanctuary. The end of it shall be with a flood, And till the end of the war desolations are determined. Then he shall confirm a covenant with many for one week; But in the middle of the week He shall bring an end to sacrifice and offering. And on the wing of abominations shall be one who makes desolate, Even until the consummation, which is determined, Is poured out on the desolate." Daniel 9:25-27 NKJV

This is the seven year covenant that will be broken in the middle by the Abomination of Desolation. We believe that the Jews will enter this covenant with a promise that they can rebuild their temple and sacrifice again, because the temple has to go back up, and sacrifice has to start in order for it to be stopped in the middle of the seven years.

B) Sacrifice begins until cleansing

There are 2300 days from the time they start sacrificing until the cleansing. And there are 1335 days from the Abomination of Desolation to the cleansing. So from the time the sacrifice starts until the Abomination of Desolation there are $2300 - 1335 = 965$ days. If you want to start counting when it comes upon us this will be another confirmation for you that the Bible is true. The temple will apparently take 285 days to be rebuilt and prepared before the sacrifices start after the covenant is made.

Then I heard a holy one speaking; and another holy one said to that certain one who was speaking, "How long will the vision be, concerning the daily sacrifices and the transgression of desolation, the giving of both the sanctuary and the host to be trampled underfoot?" And he said to me, "For two thousand three hundred days; then the sanctuary shall be cleansed."
Daniel 8:13-14 NKJV

C) 1335 Days to Cleansing

From the Abomination of Desolation there will be 1335 days until the temple is cleansed. This puts us out of the seven years. We know that the temple will be cleansed 45 days after the return of Jesus because from the Abomination to the end of the wrath there will be 1290 days. So we then have 45 days after the wrath when the temple is cleansed.

"Blessed is he who waits, and comes to the one thousand three hundred and thirty-five days.
Daniel 12:12 NKJV

D) 1290 Days from the Abomination to the End.

There will be 1290 days from the Abomination until the end of all these things. These things that were described by the angel in the previous verses is the wrath. It says in the prophecy that this angel is explaining, that the antichrist will prosper until the wrath is accomplished. So we now know there will be 1290 days from the Abomination of Desolation to the end of the wrath. And we know that he will prosper for 42 months so we can use this, to time when he starts to rule Jerusalem. Let's look at these verses.

"Then the king shall do according to his own will: he shall exalt and magnify himself above every god, shall speak blasphemies against the God of gods, and shall prosper till the wrath has been accomplished; for what has been determined shall be done.
Daniel 11:36 NKJV

"And from the time that the daily sacrifice is taken away, and the abomination of desolation is set up, there shall be one thousand two hundred and ninety days.
Daniel 12:11 NKJV

And he was given a mouth speaking great things and blasphemies, and he was given authority to continue for forty-two months.
Revelation 13:5 NKJV

E) The Abomination of Desolation

Since we've already started talking about the Abomination of Desolation, let's cover it next. It is a point from which we can determine many other things. The Sixth Seal happens after it, as does the Rapture. Many of the events mentioned in the end times are measured from this point.

First, what is it? The Abomination is something that is set up at the midpoint of the last week.

Then he shall confirm a covenant with many for one week; But in the middle of the week He shall bring an end to sacrifice and offering. And on the wing of abominations shall be one who makes desolate, Even until the consummation, which is determined, Is poured out on the desolate."
Daniel 9:27 NKJV

It is something God allows as judgment for transgression.

He even exalted himself as high as the Prince of the host; and by him the daily sacrifices were taken away, and the place of His sanctuary was cast down. Because of transgression, an army was given over to the horn to oppose the daily sacrifices; and he cast truth down to the ground. He did all this and prospered.
Daniel 8:11-12 NKJV

And it has something to do with, or is shortly followed by the antichrist declaring himself god. In Daniel 12:11 the Abomination of Desolation is 'set up' and Daniel 11:31-37 we see that the Abomination of Desolation is 'placed' in the temple as the antichrist blasphemes and exalts himself above every god.

"And forces shall be mustered by him, and they shall defile the sanctuary fortress; then they shall take away the daily sacrifices, and place there the abomination of desolation.
Daniel 11:31 NKJV

"Then the king shall do according to his own will: he shall exalt and magnify himself above every god, shall speak blasphemies against the God of gods, and shall prosper till the wrath has been accomplished; for what has been determined shall be done.
Daniel 11:36 NKJV

Now look at 2 Thessalonians 2:1-4 where Paul talks about the coming of our Lord Jesus Christ and our gathering together to Him. He says: *Now, brethren, concerning the coming of our Lord Jesus Christ and our gathering together to Him, we ask you, not to be soon shaken in mind or troubled, either by spirit or by word or by letter, as if from us, as though the day of Christ had come. Let no one deceive you by any means; for that Day will not come unless the falling away comes first, and the man of sin is revealed, the son of perdition, who opposes and exalts himself above all that is called God or that is worshiped, so that he sits as God in the temple of God, showing himself that he is God. — 2 Thessalonians 2:1-4 NKJV*

This sounds like the Abomination of Desolation in Daniel. So we have another verse that shows that the Rapture (the gathering together of the saints to Christ) will not happen until after the Abomination of Desolation. Here is the clearest passage regarding this event.

"So when you see the 'abomination of desolation,' spoken of by Daniel the prophet, standing where it ought not" (let the reader understand), "then let those who are in Judea flee to the mountains… "For in those days there will be tribulation, such as has not been since the beginning of the creation which God created until this time, nor ever shall be… But in those days, after that tribulation, the sun will be darkened, and the moon will not give its light; "the stars of heaven will fall, and the powers in the heavens will be shaken. "Then they will see the Son of Man coming in the clouds with great power and glory. "And then He will send His angels, and gather together His elect from the four winds, from the farthest part of earth to the farthest part of heaven.
Mark 13:14, 19, 24-27 NKJV

F) The Seven Seals

Something to remember when we are talking about the seals. They are what is holding the scroll shut; the scroll that contains the wrath of the Lamb and of God. Picture a piece of paper literally rolled up and sealed with seven wax seals. This is what is being described. As each seal is removed in heaven, events occur on earth that lead to the opening of the scroll that contains the wrath. Remember what happens in the spiritual realm affects the physical. This isn't symbolism…. This is a spiritual event that creates, or releases, a physical event. Once this scroll is opened the wrath begins. We think that the front of the scroll contains the wrath of the Lamb (The Trumpets) and the back the wrath of God (The Bowls).

The seals start as the antichrist starts to ride. We think this may start before the covenant. The seals are released one by one but we don't have a clear timing for them so we have grouped them into the time frame we do know.

The First Seal will be the antichrist riding

○ *And I looked, and behold, a white horse. He who sat on it had a bow; and a crown was given to him, and he went out conquering and to conquer.*
Revelation 6:2 NKJV

○ *"For many will come in My name, saying, 'I am He,' and will deceive many. "But when you hear of wars and rumors of wars, do not be troubled; for such things must happen, but the end is not yet.*
Mark 13:6-7 NKJV

The Second Seal will be world-wide war

○ *Another horse, fiery red, went out. And it was granted to the one who sat on it to take peace from the earth, and that people should kill one another; and there was given to him a great sword.*
Revelation 6:4 NKJV

○ *"For nation will rise against nation, and kingdom against kingdom...*
Mark 13:8a NKJV

The Third Seal will be famine

○ *And I heard a voice in the midst of the four living creatures saying, "A quart of wheat for a denarius, and three quarts of barley for a denarius; and do not harm the oil and the wine."*
Revelation 6:6 NKJV

○ *"...And there will be earthquakes in various places, and there will be famines and troubles. These are the beginnings of sorrows.*
Mark 13:8b NKJV

The Forth Seal will be death by sword, hunger, and beasts

○ *So I looked, and behold, a pale horse. And the name of him who sat on it was Death, and Hades followed with him. And power was given to them over a fourth of the earth, to kill with sword, with hunger, with death, and by the beasts of the earth.*
Revelation 6:8 NKJV

○ *For thus says the Lord GOD: "How much more it shall be when I send My four severe judgments on Jerusalem—the sword and famine and wild beasts and pestilence—to cut off man and beast from it?*
Ezekiel 14:21 NKJV

o *"For nation will rise against nation, and kingdom against kingdom. And there will be famines, pestilences, and earthquakes in various places.*
   Matthew 24:7 NKJV

o (Note that Mark is similar but leaves out the word pestilence… so I used Matthew here. I believe the beasts might be vectors for the pestilences and wanted to include these verses to show that. Also compare it to what God says He is sending against Jerusalem during this time. Also very similar.)

The Fifth Seal is from the perspective of heaven and it shows those who are being martyred on earth

o *When He opened the fifth seal, I saw under the altar the souls of those who had been slain for the word of God and for the testimony which they held. And they cried with a loud voice, saying, "How long, O Lord, holy and true, until You judge and avenge our blood on those who dwell on the earth?" Then a white robe was given to each of them; and it was said to them that they should rest a little while longer, until both the number of their fellow servants and their brethren, who would be killed as they were, was completed.*
   Revelation 6:9-11 NKJV

o *"But when they arrest you and deliver you up, do not worry beforehand, or premeditate what you will speak. But whatever is given you in that hour, speak that; for it is not you who speak, but the Holy Spirit. "Now brother will betray brother to death, and a father his child; and children will rise up against parents and cause them to be put to death. "And you will be hated by all for My name's sake. But he who endures to the end shall be saved.*
   Mark 13:11-13 NKJV

The Sixth Seal will be the sun, moon and stars going dark as people hide from the wrath of the Lamb that is to come. At this time the 144,000 Jewish men are sealed and the saints raptured out of the tribulation appear in heaven.

○ *I looked when He opened the sixth seal, and behold, there was a great earthquake; and the sun became black as sackcloth of hair, and the moon became like blood.*
Revelation 6:12 NKJV

○ *And the kings of the earth, the great men, the rich men, the commanders, the mighty men, every slave and every free man, hid themselves in the caves and in the rocks of the mountains, and said to the mountains and rocks, "Fall on us and hide us from the face of Him who sits on the throne and from the wrath of the Lamb! "For the great day of His wrath has come, and who is able to stand?"*
Revelation 6:15-17 NKJV

○ *After these things I looked, and behold, a great multitude which no one could number, of all nations, tribes, peoples, and tongues, standing before the throne and before the Lamb, clothed with white robes, with palm branches in their hands, and crying out with a loud voice, saying, "Salvation belongs to our God who sits on the throne, and to the Lamb!"*
Revelation 7:9-10 NKJV

○ *Then one of the elders answered, saying to me, "Who are these arrayed in white robes, and where did they come from?" And I said to him, "Sir, you know." So he said to me, "These are the ones who come out of the great tribulation, and washed their robes and made them white in the blood of the Lamb.*
Revelation 7:13-14 NKJV

○ *"But in those days, after that tribulation, the sun will be darkened, and the moon will not give its light; "the stars of heaven will fall, and the powers in the heavens will be shaken. "Then they will see the Son of Man coming in the clouds with great power and glory. "And then He will send His angels, and gather together His elect from the four winds, from the farthest part of earth to the farthest part of heaven.*
Mark 13:24-27 NKJV

○ Please note that the sealed are specifically from Israel, they are alive at the time of the sealing, and they are virgin males… the great multitude is from every tribe, people and tongue and they are gathered from both heaven and earth. Please don't confuse these two groups.

The Seventh Seal the Trumpets are given to seven angels and fire is thrown to the earth.

○ *When He opened the seventh seal, there was silence in heaven for about half an hour. And I saw the seven angels who stand before God, and to them were given seven trumpets. Then another angel, having a golden censer, came and stood at the altar. He was given much incense, that he should offer it with the prayers of all the saints upon the golden altar which was before the throne. And the smoke of the incense, with the prayers of the saints, ascended before God from the angel's hand. Then the angel took the censer, filled it with fire from the altar, and threw it to the earth. And there were noises, thunderings, lightnings, and an earthquake. So the seven angels who had the seven trumpets prepared themselves to sound.*
Revelation 8:1-6 NKJV

 Please take a moment to go and read Mark 13 (or Matthew 24, or Luke 21) and Revelation 6-7 completely and compare these seals with what Jesus says. You will see that He warns them of the seals in the order that they happen in Revelation. Then in verse 14 He warns of the Abomination of Desolation and tells all in Judea to flee. This will start a short period called the Great Tribulation. This is the same time that 'those who have understanding' according to Daniel are going to be martyred.

"And forces shall be mustered by him, and they shall defile the sanctuary fortress; then they shall take away the daily sacrifices, and place there the abomination of desolation. "Those who do wickedly against the covenant he shall corrupt with flattery; but the people who know their God shall be strong, and carry out great exploits. "And those of the people who understand shall instruct many; yet for many days they shall fall by sword and flame, by captivity and plundering. — Daniel 11:31-33 NKJV

This Great Tribulation ends with the Rapture of the Church and the remnant of Israel being carried on Eagles Wings into the wilderness to be nourished for 42 months. These are the Jews who turn to God after they look on 'Him who they pierced' when He comes for us in the clouds.

See the sections in the Rapture and the Woman Nourished for more information.

G) The Great Tribulation

The Great Tribulation and the time of Jacob's trouble.

The Great Tribulation will happen to the Church, and after we are raptured, the Jews who begin to believe will face the time of Jacob's trouble. First the Great Tribulation.

After the Abomination of Desolation there will be a time of persecution and tribulation like never before. This time won't end until we are raptured.

*"So when you see the 'abomination of desolation,' spoken of by Daniel the prophet, standing where it ought not" (let the reader understand), "then let those who are in Judea flee to the mountains. ... "For in those days there will be tribulation, such as has not been since the beginning of the creation which God created until this time, nor ever shall be. "And unless the Lord had shortened those days, no flesh would be saved; but for the elect's sake, whom He chose, He shortened the days. ... "But in those days, after that tribulation, the sun will be darkened, and the moon will not give its light; "the stars of heaven will fall, and the powers in the heavens will be shaken. "Then they will see the Son of Man coming in the clouds with great power and glory.
Mark 13:14, 19-20, 24-26 NKJV*

This is the time that Daniel spoke of when he said: "And those of the people who understand shall instruct many; yet for many days they shall fall by sword and flame, by captivity and plundering. - Daniel 11:33 NKJV

If you think that because Jesus loves you, He won't let you go through hard times, then you need to consider what the Bible says about going through tribulation.

Daniel continues: *"And some of those of understanding shall fall, to refine them, purify them, and make them white, until the time of the end; because it is still for the appointed time. - Daniel 11:35 NKJV*

Paul tells us that tribulation is spiritually good for us: *And not only that, but we also glory in tribulations, knowing that tribulation produces perseverance; and perseverance, character; and character, hope. Now hope does not disappoint, because the love of God has been poured out in our hearts by the Holy Spirit who was given to us. - Romans 5:3-5 NKJV*

Jesus says: *"These things I have spoken to you, that in Me you may have peace. In the world you will have tribulation; but be of good cheer, I have overcome the world." - John 16:33 NKJV*

Paul asks: *"Who shall separate us from the love of Christ? Shall tribulation, or distress, or persecution, or famine, or nakedness, or peril, or sword? - Romans 8:35 NKJV*

In Revelation Jesus warns: *"Do not fear any of those things which you are about to suffer. Indeed, the devil is about to throw some of you into prison, that you may be tested, and you will have tribulation ten days. Be faithful until death, and I will give you the crown of life. - Revelation 2:10 NKJV*

But we know that it ends well for when we have endured to the end we will be saved: *"And I said to him, "Sir, you know." So he said to me, "These are the ones who come out of the great tribulation, and washed their robes and made them white in the blood of the Lamb. - Revelation 7:14 NKJV*

This next passage also describes the Great Tribulation but from Luke. What is different is that it mentions the armies (that Daniel also mentions when he talks about the setting up of the Abomination of Desolation) surrounding the city. Then it describes how there will be great distress in the land and wrath upon this people (the Jewish people). He says they will fall by the sword and be led away captive into all nations. Read it carefully because we will see this in the time of Jacob's trouble.

"But when you see Jerusalem surrounded by armies, then know that its desolation is near. "Then let those who are in Judea flee to the mountains, let those who are in the midst of her depart, and let not those who are in the country enter her. "For these are the days of vengeance, that all things which are written may be fulfilled. "But woe to those who are pregnant and to those who are nursing babies in those days! For there will be great distress in the land and wrath upon this people. "And they will fall by the edge of the sword, and be led away captive into all nations. And Jerusalem will be trampled by Gentiles until the times of the Gentiles are fulfilled.
Luke 21:20-24 NKJV

Now when we are raptured, the dragon turns his wrath on the people in Israel. The armies surrounding the city eventually win and the people are carried into captivity.

She bore a male Child who was to rule all nations with a rod of iron. And her Child was caught up (this is harpazo – rapture –the same word used in 1 Thessalonians 4:17) *to God and His throne. Then the woman fled into the wilderness, where she has a place prepared by God, that they should feed her there one thousand two hundred and sixty days. ... So the great dragon was cast out, that serpent of old, called the devil and Satan, who deceives the whole world; he was cast to the earth, and his angels were cast out with him. Then I heard a loud voice saying in heaven, "Now salvation, and strength, and the kingdom of our God, and the power of His Christ have come, for the accuser of our brethren, who accused them before our God day and night, has been cast down. And they overcame him by the blood of the Lamb and by the word of their testimony, and they did not love their lives to the death. "Therefore rejoice, O heavens, and you who dwell in them! Woe to the inhabitants of the earth and the sea! For the devil has come down to you, having great wrath, because he knows that he has a short time."*
Revelation 12:5-6, 9-12 NKJV

Satan was cast out of heaven and he is furious. He persecutes the woman with all of this rage. This is the time of Jacob's trouble. The time that Jacob will be saved out of.

Now these are the words that the LORD spoke concerning Israel and Judah. "*For thus says the LORD: 'We have heard a voice of trembling, Of fear, and not of peace. Ask now, and see, Whether a man is ever in labor with*

child? So why do I see every man with his hands on his loins Like a woman in labor, And all faces turned pale? Alas! For that day is great, So that none is like it; And it is the time of Jacob's trouble, But he shall be saved out of it. 'For it shall come to pass in that day,' Says the LORD of hosts, 'That I will break his yoke from your neck, And will burst your bonds; Foreigners shall no more enslave them.
Jeremiah 30:4-8 NKJV

'Therefore do not fear, O My servant Jacob,' says the LORD, 'Nor be dismayed, O Israel; For behold, I will save you from afar, And your seed from the land of their captivity. Jacob shall return, have rest and be quiet, And no one shall make him afraid. For I am with you,' says the LORD, 'to save you; Though I make a full end of all nations where I have scattered you, Yet I will not make a complete end of you. But I will correct you in justice, And will not let you go altogether unpunished.' ... The fierce anger of the LORD will not return until He has done it, And until He has performed the intents of His heart. In the latter days you will consider it.
Jeremiah 30:10-11, 24 NKJV

"At the same time," says the LORD, "I will be the God of all the families of Israel, and they shall be My people." Thus says the LORD: "The people who survived the sword found grace in the wilderness--Israel, when I went to give him rest." The LORD has appeared of old to me, saying: "Yes, I have loved you with an everlasting love; Therefore with lovingkindness I have drawn you.
Jeremiah 31:1-3 NKJV

Please note that this is a time of severe trouble for Israel but that God saves them out of it, and that those who survive the sword find grace and rest in the wilderness. This time lasts less than 30 days for those of Israel who find grace and rest.

Those who survive will look at Jesus when He returns for us in the clouds and realize that they were wrong about the Messiah. They will repent but they will have missed the Rapture. These are the remnant of Israel.

Behold, He is coming with clouds, and every eye will see Him, even they who pierced Him. And all the tribes of the earth will mourn because of Him. Even so, Amen.

Revelation 1:7 NKJV

"And I will pour on the house of David and on the inhabitants of Jerusalem the Spirit of grace and supplication; then they will look on Me whom they pierced. Yes, they will mourn for Him as one mourns for his only son, and grieve for Him as one grieves for a firstborn. "In that day there shall be a great mourning in Jerusalem, like the mourning at Hadad Rimmon in the plain of Megiddo. Zechariah 12:10-11 NKJV

Now back to the timeline. If they will look at the one they have pierced and mourn in Israel, then there will be a multitude who are saved but not Raptured. These are the remnant that God nourishes in the wilderness. Please note Jerimiah 30-31 above where it says that God won't leave them unpunished but that those who survive find 'grace in the wilderness.' This proves that the woman in the wilderness is Israel.

H) The Rapture

If you skipped to this section to see if our explanation of the Rapture matches what you already believe then please take a second to remove your denominational glasses. Sometimes we don't even realize that we have put them back on. We will support every view that we share with Bible verses.

First the Rapture

For the Lord Himself will descend from heaven with a shout, with the voice of an archangel, and with the trumpet of God. And the dead in Christ will rise first. Then we who are alive and remain shall be caught up together with them in the clouds to meet the Lord in the air. And thus we shall always be with the Lord. Therefore comfort one another with these words.
1 Thessalonians 4:16-18 NKJV

But when does this happen?

Paul explains in 2 Thessalonians 2:1-4 where he talks about the coming of our Lord Jesus Christ and our gathering together to Him.

He says: *Now, brethren, concerning the coming of our Lord Jesus Christ and our gathering together to Him, we ask you, not to be soon shaken in mind or troubled, either by spirit or by word or by letter, as if from us, as though the day of Christ had come. Let no one deceive you by any means; for that Day will not come unless the falling away comes first, and the man of sin is revealed, the son of perdition, who opposes and exalts himself above all that is called God or that is worshiped, so that he sits as God in the temple of God, showing himself that he is God. — 2 Thessalonians 2:1-4 NKJV*

This sounds like the Abomination of Desolation in Daniel. (If you haven't read it already please read point E the Abomination.) So this verse shows that the Rapture (the gathering together of the saints to Christ) will not happen until after the Abomination of Desolation. Then there is Mathew 24 and Mark 13, both the same account that say that after the tribulation of those days He will come in the clouds for us. The tribulation of those days starts after the Abomination of Desolation. Read this in Mark 13. Please go read it for yourself so you can see the verses we left out because it was too long, and understand that this is all one concept.

"So when you see the 'abomination of desolation,' spoken of by Daniel the prophet, standing where it ought not" (let the reader understand), "then let those who are in Judea flee to the mountains. ... "For in those days there will be tribulation, such as has not been since the beginning of the creation which God created until this time, nor ever shall be. ... "But in those days, after that tribulation, the sun will be darkened, and the moon will not give its light; "the stars of heaven will fall, and the powers in the heavens will be shaken. "Then they will see the Son of Man coming in the clouds with great power and glory. "And then He will send His angels, and gather together His elect from the four winds, from the farthest part of earth to the farthest part of heaven. Mark 13:14, 19, 24-27 NKJV

So we know it happens after the Abomination and that there will be a period of Great Tribulation before we go. We also know that the Rapture happens in the Sixth Seal (if you missed that then go read the sixth seal section of the seals Part F).

So we know that it happens in the Sixth Seal, but when is the sixth seal? The next section will be about the woman clothed with the sun in Revelation 12 and we will get into it further there, but we know that the Rapture happens before the woman is taken to the wilderness by the Eagles Wings. This period lasts for 42 months, until the end of the Wrath. So we know that the Sixth Seal and the Rapture happen at some point in the 30 days between the Abomination and the Woman being carried to the wilderness.

I) Woman Nourished

Please turn to Revelation 12 if you want to better understand this explanation. The chapter is too long to include here. Here is the main verse that describes the woman.

Now a great sign appeared in heaven: a woman clothed with the sun, with the moon under her feet, and on her head a garland of twelve stars.
Revelation 12:1 NKJV

First of all, who is the woman? I'll give you a hint, her name isn't Mary. The woman described here is clothed in the sun, has the moon at her feet, and twelve stars on her head. Now, to understand who she is we need to see in the Bible if we can find the sun and the moon and twelve stars.

Then he dreamed still another dream and told it to his brothers, and said, "Look, I have dreamed another dream. And this time, the sun, the moon, and the eleven stars bowed down to me."
Genesis 37:9 NKJV

But the dream of Joseph had only eleven stars. This is because Joseph is one of the twelve sons of Israel and in his dream his father (the sun), his mother (the moon), and his eleven brothers (the stars) are bowing to him.

Because the Bible explains the Bible, we can see that the woman in Revelation 12 must be the nation of Israel. This explanation also makes more sense in the context of the verse.

The rest of this passage says that she gave birth to a male child who would rule the nations with an iron rod, the dragon was waiting at her feet to devour the child, the child was then caught up to heaven and the dragon persecuted the woman.

At first glance people think the woman is Mary and the male child Jesus, but this doesn't work. First, Jesus was not 'caught up' to heaven. This is a snatching away and if you remember in Acts; Jesus ascended in the cloud and the angel promised He would return in the same way. The word caught up is used to describe the Rapture of the church in 1 Thessalonians 4:17. Second, Mary was not persecuted after Jesus' ascension. In Revelation Jesus promises overcomers in the Church that they will rule with an iron rod.

"And he who overcomes, and keeps My works until the end, to him I will give power over the nations. He shall rule them with a rod of iron; They shall be dashed to pieces like the potter's vessels'--as I also have received from My Father; Revelation 2:26-27 NKJV

The woman is Israel and here we, the Church (the body of Christ), are the male child who is caught up. After we are caught up Revelation 12 says that the dragon persecuted the woman, but that she was carried on Eagles Wings where she is nourished for time, time and half a time. This is three and a half years. In another verse it says that she will be nourished for 1,260 days. Also equal to three and a half years or 42 months.

Then the woman fled into the wilderness, where she has a place prepared by God, that they should feed her there one thousand two hundred and sixty days. Revelation 12:6 NKJV

But the woman was given two wings of a great eagle, that she might fly into the wilderness to her place, where she is nourished for a time and times and half a time, from the presence of the serpent. Revelation 12:14 NKJV

We know that the dragon persecutes Israel after the Rapture. We know that the Rapture doesn't occur until after the Abomination of Desolation. We know that after the Abomination of Desolation there is a time when Christians will be persecuted. The Great Tribulation.

"And those of the people who understand shall instruct many; yet for many days they shall fall by sword and flame, by captivity and plundering.
Daniel 11:33 NKJV

This time is short. Less than 30 days on our time line because the 1,290 days from the Abomination of Desolation until the end, combined with the 1,260 days that the woman will be nourished, only leaves 30 days. In this 30 days the Church will be persecuted, then Raptured, then the dragon will go after Israel. This period where the dragon persecutes Israel is also called the time of Jacob's Trouble. Please see the Great Tribulation section for more information on this.

We also see that if there are 'many days' between the Abomination of Desolation and the woman being carried away, that to fulfill the full 1,260 days she has to be in the wilderness beyond the 7 year covenant.

J) The Antichrist Given Authority

For the same period of time as the woman is nourished in the wilderness, the antichrist will be given authority to speak blasphemies and tread the holy city underfoot.

And he was given a mouth speaking great things and blasphemies, and he was given authority to continue for forty-two months. Then he opened his mouth in blasphemy against God, to blaspheme His name, His tabernacle, and those who dwell in heaven. It was granted to him to make war with the saints and to overcome them. And authority was given him over every tribe, tongue, and nation. All who dwell on the earth will worship him, whose names have not been written in the Book of Life of the Lamb slain from the foundation of the world.
Revelation 13:5-8 NKJV

He shall speak pompous words against the Most High, Shall persecute the saints of the Most High, And shall intend to change times and law. Then the saints shall be given into his hand For a time and times and half a time.
Daniel 7:25 NKJV

Note: These saints are the ones who come to Christ either when they see the Rapture or after the Rapture. There are many, many lukewarm Christians in this world, there are many more who are backslidden and living in sin. They will repent when they see that they are left behind. They know the truth but they weren't living it. They will be killed by the antichrist for a time, times and half a time. Please don't be one of these. Please make sure that your life is right with God. Please examine yourself and examine your Bible to see if you're living in a way that pleases God.

"But leave out the court which is outside the temple, and do not measure it, for it has been given to the Gentiles. And they will tread the holy city underfoot for forty-two months.
Revelation 11:2 NKJV

All these verses speak of the same time frame. A time when the antichrist has authority to blaspheme God, prevail against the saints (those who are saved after the Rapture), and tread the holy city underfoot. In Daniel we are told that this happens until the wrath is complete.

"Then the king shall do according to his own will: he shall exalt and magnify himself above every god, shall speak blasphemies against the God of gods, and shall prosper till the wrath has been accomplished; for what has been determined shall be done.
Daniel 11:36 NKJV

So we see this time period (like the time that the woman is nourished) must start thirty days after the Abomination of Desolation and last until the end of the wrath, 1290 days after the Abomination of Desolation.

K) The Two Witnesses

And I will give power to my two witnesses, and they will prophesy one thousand two hundred and sixty days, clothed in sackcloth."

Revelation 11:3 NKJV

The Two Witnesses will come to prophesy for the same amount of time that the Holy City will be tread underfoot by the antichrist. We believe that they will start their prophecies a few days before the abomination that causes desolation. This is because they have to preach for 42 months (1,260 days), then lie in the streets for 3.5 days until they are raised. They are raised right before the seventh trumpet, so they are on the earth at least 1,263.5 days before the seventh trumpet sounds and the seven year covenant ends. This places their arrival just before the Abomination.

We, the Christians, will have the chance to see them and hear them right before the Rapture. We're not sure for how long, because we don't have an exact date for the Rapture, but they may start their ministry encouraging the Church of Christ.

It makes complete sense that they preach during the second half of the Seven Years because the Christians will be gone. They will give the Jewish people and the world a chance to repent of their wickedness and turn to God. We don't know exactly what they will say or preach but the Bible says they will prophesy and give testimony.

And if anyone wants to harm them, fire proceeds from their mouth and devours their enemies. And if anyone wants to harm them, he must be killed in this manner. These have power to shut heaven, so that no rain falls in the days of their prophecy; and they have power over waters to turn them to blood, and to strike the earth with all plagues, as often as they desire.
Revelation 11:5-6 NKJV

The Two Witnesses will have power to perform mighty signs and to defend themselves against their enemies with deadly force. They will try to get the whole world's attention with different plagues and with judgment.

They won't be able to die until the days of their prophecies are over. Then the antichrist will be able to kill them. They will be dead for three and a half days.

When they finish their testimony, the beast that ascends out of the bottomless pit will make war against them, overcome them, and kill them. And their dead bodies will lie in the street of the great city which spiritually is called Sodom and Egypt, where also our Lord was crucified. Then those from the peoples, tribes, tongues, and nations will see their dead bodies three-and-a-half days, and not allow their dead bodies to be put into graves.
Revelation 11:7-9 NKJV

All this will occur in Israel, and the whole world will see their bodies. This is possible now with the technology that we have like satellites, internet and cellphones. The world will celebrate their death because they tormented them for 1260 days. But after three and a half days the Two Witnesses will come to life and they will ascend to heaven in a cloud. We believe they will die between the Sixth and Seventh Trumpets and they will rise again the same day the Seventh Trumpet sounds.

Who are the Two Witnesses? The Bible doesn't mention clearly who they are. But we believe that they are Enoch and Elijah because they are the only ones that didn't die.

And as it is appointed for men to die once, but after this the judgment,
Hebrews 9:27 NKJV

All men and women have to die before the time is over. Both of them were prophets in their time. Jesus says that Elijah will come back (Matthew 17:11) but the Bible doesn't say for sure, so if you see two guys clothed in sackcloth in Jerusalem preaching and burning people with the fire of their mouth you will know it's them. If you see their bodies lying for three and a half days, I'm sorry but you have the mark of the beast.

L) The Seven Trumpets

(Note for those who missed the Rapture)
I want to start this point in the timeline with a very serious warning. At this moment in the last Seven Years the Rapture just happened.

From this point forward the Wrath of the Lamb will start, and the whole world will be judged, including the brand new Christians and the former backsliders.

If you saw all the signs before the Rapture given in this book you missed it. If you see the Son of Man in the clouds and you don't rise to meet Him you missed it. If you see people in your life who you knew were good with God just disappear; then you must repent right now!

Yes, there is salvation in Christ after the Rapture but the coming time will be of tremendous terror and suffering. My hope is that this book finds you before it is too late to prepare; but my prayer is that you find Jesus before it is too late.

Now, the Seven Trumpets are what the Bible calls the Wrath of the Lamb (Revelation 6:16-17). The Lamb will avenge His Bride because of what the world will do to her.

and said to the mountains and rocks, "Fall on us and hide us from the face of Him who sits on the throne and from the wrath of the Lamb! For the great day of His wrath has come, and who is able to stand?"
Revelation 6:16-17 NKJV

First to Third Trumpets

The first angel sounded: And hail and fire followed, mingled with blood, and they were thrown to the earth. And a third of the trees were burned up, and all green grass was burned up.
Revelation 8:7 NKJV

Then the second angel sounded: And something like a great mountain burning with fire was thrown into the sea, and a third of the sea became blood. And a third of the living creatures in the sea died, and a third of the ships were destroyed.
Revelation 8:8-9 NKJV

Then the third angel sounded: And a great star fell from heaven, burning like a torch, and it fell on a third of the rivers and on the springs of water. The name of the star is Wormwood. A third of the waters became wormwood, and many men

died from the water, because it was made bitter.
Revelation 8:10-11 NKJV

I believe these three Trumpets will bring destruction by one single event, an Asteroid. Let's go back to Revelation 6 to understand something.

And the kings of the earth, the great men, the rich men, the commanders, the mighty men, every slave and every free man, hid themselves in the caves and in the rocks of the mountains, and said to the mountains and rocks, "Fall on us and hide us from the face of Him who sits on the throne and from the wrath of the Lamb! For the great day of His wrath has come, and who is able to stand?"
Revelation 6:15-17 NKJV

They hide in caves and in the rocks because they see something coming that requires them to hide. Understand this, there are many underground bunkers around the world built from the Cold War until today. Many more are being built right now, so this point makes a lot of sense.

The destruction that is mentioned is not symbolic, it will actually happen. Just take a moment and search for videos about the destruction that an Asteroid can cause to the Earth. I'm pretty sure that the nations will try to destroy it before it gets too close like in that movie... I think that this will make it worse, and that is why it will come as three waves.

If you notice, all of the first three Trumpets will affect one third of the Earth. I believe that it will be the same third of the planet getting hit three times. Which part of the planet? We don't know but let's consider this:

There is an Asteroid named Apophis that will pass very close to the Earth in 2029. NASA originally predicted that Apophis would hit the Earth but now, of course, they say it will miss us. But we need to remember our history. Just in 2020 the "experts" said many things about what we went through that we now know were lies. They lie to "protect us" so of course they won't say now that an Asteroid will hit us. Many experts say that it is way too early and too far to know for a fact that it will miss us in 2029. But also they agree that if Apophis misses us in 2029 it will be more likely to hit us in 2036. A seven year cycle. You can read more on https://solarsystem.nasa.gov/asteroids-comets-and-meteors/asteroids/apophis/in-depth/

 I'm not saying that the Asteroid Apophis is the Wormwood of Revelation 8. I AM NOT SETTING DATES but this is real proof that the events of the first three Trumpets are possible without going too deep in the supernatural. This isn't something we can be sure of but it's definitely a possibility.

Note: Apophis means god of chaos. A demon serpent from Egyptian mythology. It will be the closest to the Earth on April, Friday the 13th of 2029 at 6:00pm.

The Fourth Trumpet

Then the fourth angel sounded: And a third of the sun was struck, a third of the moon, and a third of the stars, so that a third of them were darkened. A third of the day did not shine, and likewise the night.
Revelation 8:12 NKJV

We can't really explain what could cause this next event, but because we just proved that the first three events are naturally possible there's no reason to believe this event will be symbolic. It seems like this will affect the whole world and it's different from when the sun darkens and the moon becomes like blood. Either there is something that makes the sun, moon, and stars appear dark from one third of the Earth or God literally strikes all three sources of light and diminishes their light by one third. If you ask me to guess, my best guess is: I don't know.

 If you happen to miss the Rapture I think you'd like to have been in the third part of the world that was already destroyed, because of the horror of the last three Trumpets.

And I looked, and I heard an angel flying through the midst of heaven, saying with a loud voice, "Woe, woe, woe to the inhabitants of the earth, because of the

remaining blasts of the trumpet of the three angels who are about to sound!"
Revelation 8:13 NKJV

The Fifth Trumpet

Then the fifth angel sounded: And I saw a star fallen from heaven to the earth.
To him was given the key to the bottomless pit. And he opened the bottomless pit,
and smoke arose out of the pit like the smoke of a great furnace. So the sun and
the air were darkened because of the smoke of the pit. Then out of the smoke
locusts came upon the earth. And to them was given power, as the scorpions of the
earth have power. They were commanded not to harm the grass of the earth, or
any green thing, or any tree, but only those men who do not have the seal of God
on their foreheads. And they were not given authority to kill them, but to torment
them for five months. Their torment was like the torment of a scorpion when it
strikes a man. In those days men will seek death and will not find it; they will
desire to die, and death will flee from them.
Revelation 9:1-6 NKJV

This star that falls from heaven isn't an actual star nor an Asteroid.
It's an angel of some sort because the pronouns "to him" and "he".
He will have the key to the bottomless pit in the Earth and he will
release the "locusts," but not real ones. I believe they are like angels
that are to torment the people of the Earth. I say angels because they
have an angel as their king. Remember, not all angels are nice.

And they had as king over them the angel of the bottomless pit, whose name in
Hebrew is Abaddon, but in Greek he has the name Apollyon.
Revelation 9:11 NKJV

Read Revelation 9:1-11 carefully because people who believe in Post
Tribulation Rapture believe that the Christians will be protected
during this time. In verse 4, it says that the creatures are commanded
to harm those men (women included) who do not have the seal of
God on their foreheads. The only ones who have the seal of God on
their foreheads are the 144,000 from the tribes of Israel. Also
remember that the woman of Revelation 12 (the believing remnant of
Israel) is out of the rest of the End Times picture. She's being
protected and nourished by God.

So for five months the locusts will "torture" all men. Let me make this clear. It isn't that all men will be tortured during the five months, but the creatures will have authority for five months. Maybe some will suffer for a few weeks and some for a few months but everyone will be tortured. Maybe it will be like a plague, or maybe they'll actually see these spiritual creatures moving from house to house, but whatever they are it will be very, very bad.

The Sixth Trumpet

Then the sixth angel sounded: And I heard a voice from the four horns of the golden altar which is before God, saying to the sixth angel who had the trumpet, "Release the four angels who are bound at the great river Euphrates." So the four angels, who had been prepared for the hour and day and month and year, were released to kill a third of mankind.
Revelation 9:13-15 NKJV

This time there are four angels that will be in charge of killing one third of mankind. These are not the same kind of angel that we are used to when we read the Bible. They are bound on Earth at the Euphrates. They were prepared to kill and make judgments.

Don't think that they will kill a third of the people that we have in the world today. Remember that before we got to this point we had great wars, great earthquakes, famines, pestilences, the Rapture and the first three Trumpets. So the population is much smaller at this point in the End Times.

Next, one of the most misinterpreted End Time events.
Now the number of the army of the horsemen was two hundred million; I heard the number of them.
Revelation 9:16 NKJV

The common interpretation of this verse is that an army of 200,000,000 soldiers will surround Israel to attack them. Well, this is nothing like that at all. They said that China has an army that is this big, or maybe Russia. Let's entertain that bad interpretation for a moment. Yes, China's army could be that big and maybe Russia's army too. But again, those armies will be hit very hard by the great wars, great earthquakes, famines, pestilences, the Rapture, and the bitter waters. So then their armies won't be that big.

Also John saw horses not things like horses. I'm pretty sure he knew what a horse looks like, but those horses have heads like lions and tails like serpents. Each one of the horsemen has their own horse. There are not 200 million horses in the world today, much less at that point in the End Times.

And the idea that a 200 million man army will cross from China to Israel on foot, sorry on horseback, is crazy enough. But more crazy than that, is that this army could kill one third of mankind from where they are gathered in Israel with fire, smoke and brimstone that is coming out of the mouths of those horses.

The angels that are released have an army of angels with them. The text doesn't say they came from a foreign land, so the 200 million horsemen are the spiritual forces commanded by the first four angels.

Also, the four angels are leading this great army to kill people by plagues.

By these three plagues a third of mankind was killed—by the fire and the smoke and the brimstone which came out of their mouths. For their power is in their mouth and in their tails; for their tails are like serpents, having heads; and with them they do harm.
Revelation 9:18-19 NKJV

Their power is in their mouth and their tails, tails like a serpent. These can be creatures that were created for this specific task. The Bible doesn't say if those are evil or good angels so we don't know. Some believe that they are fallen angels, but again we don't know. They will bring plagues of fire, smoke and brimstone. That's all we know about them.

Listen to what Joel describes:

A day of darkness and gloominess, A day of clouds and thick darkness, Like the morning clouds spread over the mountains. A people come, great and strong, The like of whom has never been; Nor will there ever be any such after them, Even for many successive generations. A fire devours before them, And behind them a flame burns; The land is like the Garden of Eden before them, And behind them a desolate wilderness; Surely nothing shall escape them. Their appearance is like the appearance of horses; And like swift steeds, so they run. With a noise like chariots Over mountaintops they leap, Like the noise of a flaming fire that devours the stubble, Like a strong people set in battle array. Before them the people writhe in pain; All faces are drained of color. They run like mighty men, They climb the wall like men of war; Every one marches in formation, And they do not break ranks. They do not push one another; Every one marches in his own column. Though they lunge between the weapons, They are not cut down. They run to and fro in the city, They run on the wall; They climb into the houses, They enter at the windows like a thief.
Joel 2:2-9 NKJV

This sounds very similar to the 200,000,000 creature army described above. People writhe in pain before they come and there is darkness and gloominess like when the smoke from the pit darkens the sky (Trumpet 5) and they destroy with fire. Note they lunge between weapons and aren't cut down. This means they can't just be symbolic.

And finally, God blew my mind when He brought this verse to me. For those who still don't believe that John is seeing into the spiritual world, read this.

And Elisha prayed, and said, "Lord, I pray, open his eyes that he may see." Then the Lord opened the eyes of the young man, and he saw. And behold, the mountain was full of horses and chariots of fire all around Elisha.
II Kings 6:17 NKJV

Elisha and the young man saw an army that filled the mountain with HORSES and chariots of fire! John was seeing into the spiritual not the physical world at this time. Remember though that spiritual beings can act in the physical realm. Remember the angels that were in Sodom and Gomorrah... they physically pulled Lot into the house and blinded the evil men. So don't start thinking that what is being described won't physically happen just because it has a spiritual cause.

Now one third of mankind was killed in this trumpet, and I believe that this is the end of any of the post-rapture Christians that were left, because of the next verse.

But the rest of mankind, who were not killed by these plagues, did not repent of the works of their hands, that they should not worship demons, and idols of gold, silver, brass, stone, and wood, which can neither see nor hear nor walk. And they did not repent of their murders or their sorceries or their sexual immorality or their thefts.
Revelation 9:20-21 NKJV

The rest of mankind, the ones who survived, didn't repent. So now the world is full of evil, sexually immoral, thieves and demon worshippers. They are about to feel the weight of the Wrath of God. And yes, it gets much worse.

Note: The Sixth Trumpet ends with the raising and ascension of The Two Witnesses.

The mighty angel with a little book

This is very important to understand. All this is happening in the spirit. But this chapter is key for understanding that the time of the last Seven Years, or the Seventieth Week of Daniel, and the Time of the Gentiles is about to end.

I saw still another mighty angel coming down from heaven, clothed with a cloud. And a rainbow was on his head, his face was like the sun, and his feet like pillars of fire. He had a little book open in his hand. And he set his right foot on the sea and his left foot on the land, and cried with a loud voice, as when a lion roars. When he cried out, seven thunders uttered their voices. Now when the seven thunders uttered their voices, I was about to write; but I heard a voice from heaven saying to me, "Seal up the things which the seven thunders uttered, and do not write them." The angel whom I saw standing on the sea and on the land raised up his hand to heaven and swore by Him who lives forever and ever, who created heaven and the things that are in it, the earth and the things that are in it, and the sea and the things that are in it, that there should be delay no longer, but in the days of the sounding of the seventh angel, when he is about to sound, the

mystery of God would be finished, as He declared to His servants the prophets.
Revelation 10:1-7 NKJV

It is good to point out that all this is happening right before the last Trumpet sounds. This mighty angel, one who we can't be sure of his identity, comes down from heaven. Some people believe that he can be Jesus himself because the description given in Revelation 10 is very similar to Ezekiel 1:26.

The important thing is the proclamation that this angel makes.

and swore by Him who lives forever and ever, who created heaven and the things that are in it, the earth and the things that are in it, and the sea and the things that are in it, that there should be delay no longer, but in the days of the sounding of the seventh angel, when he is about to sound, the mystery of God would be finished, as He declared to His servants the prophets.
Revelation 10:6-7 NKJV

This angel swore by God! That's a very big deal. He swore that at the sound of the Seventh Trumpet that the mystery of God would be finished! It's over. The time of this world will come to an end. How do we know that? It's revealed in the Seventh Trumpet.

The Seventh Trumpet

Then the seventh angel sounded: And there were loud voices in heaven, saying, "The kingdoms of this world have become the kingdoms of our Lord and of His Christ, and He shall reign forever and ever!"
Revelation 11:15 NKJV

The kingdoms of this world are now the kingdoms of God! The time of the Gentiles is over. The last Seven Years are over. Now Jesus is the King of this world and soon He will return to establish His kingdom and to clean up the mess and the evil that is left. There is a great celebration in heaven because of God taking back His kingdom. They are having a party in heaven!

And the twenty-four elders who sat before God on their thrones fell on their faces and worshiped God, saying: "We give You thanks, O Lord God Almighty, The

One who is and who was and who is to come, Because You have taken Your great power and reigned. The nations were angry, and Your wrath has come, And the time of the dead, that they should be judged, And that You should reward Your servants the prophets and the saints, And those who fear Your name, small and great, And should destroy those who destroy the earth." Then the temple of God was opened in heaven, and the ark of His covenant was seen in His temple. And there were lightnings, noises, thunderings, an earthquake, and great hail.
Revelation 11:16-19 NKJV

Now the worst of the Wrath of God will be poured out and the saints will be rewarded. In our timeline, from this moment until Jesus returns will be 30 days.

M) The Seven Bowls of the Wrath of God

Then I saw another sign in heaven, great and marvelous: seven angels having the seven last plagues, for in them the wrath of God is complete. And I saw something like a sea of glass mingled with fire, and those who have the victory over the beast, over his image and over his mark and over the number of his name, standing on the sea of glass, having harps of God.
Revelation 15:1-2 NKJV

The Apostle John saw this before the Wrath of God was poured out. These groups of people are the ones who die during the time of the Seven Trumpets. They have the victory over the beast which means they chose to die before they would worship him or take his mark. There is no second Rapture. Everyone who was left behind after the Sixth Seal and got saved after, had to die before this time. At this point we are certain there are no Christians left except those directly protected by God (the 144,000 and the Woman being nourished).

Then I heard a loud voice from the temple saying to the seven angels, "Go and pour out the bowls of the wrath of God on the earth."
Revelation 16:1 NKJV

The First Bowl

So the first went and poured out his bowl upon the earth, and a foul and

loathsome sore came upon the men who had the mark of the beast and those who worshiped his image.
Revelation 16:2 NKJV

This is self-explanatory.

The Second Bowl

Then the second angel poured out his bowl on the sea, and it became blood as of a dead man; and every living creature in the sea died.
Revelation 16:3 NKJV

This time God is not affecting the waters only, but killing every creature that is in the water.

The Third Bowl

Then the third angel poured out his bowl on the rivers and springs of water, and they became blood. And I heard the angel of the waters saying: "You are righteous, O Lord, The One who is and who was and who is to be, Because You have judged these things. For they have shed the blood of saints and prophets, And You have given them blood to drink. For it is their just due."
Revelation 16:4-6 NKJV

Now all water will be contaminated, and from here on mankind won't last very long because of the lack of clean water. This fits into the last 30 days of our timeline.

The Fourth Bowl

Then the fourth angel poured out his bowl on the sun, and power was given to him to scorch men with fire. And men were scorched with great heat, and they blasphemed the name of God who has power over these plagues; and they did not repent and give Him glory.
Revelation 16:8-9 NKJV

This is another reason why I said nobody will get saved in this period. This angel will cause something like a sun storm that will create solar flares and cause great heat. But as Pharaoh refused to repent in the time of Moses, these people don't repent!

The Fifth Bowl

Then the fifth angel poured out his bowl on the throne of the beast, and his kingdom became full of darkness; and they gnawed their tongues because of the pain. They blasphemed the God of heaven because of their pains and their sores, and did not repent of their deeds.
Revelation 16:10-11 NKJV

One more time they refused to repent! I believe that they'd still have a chance to repent if they were willing. That's why it's mentioned again. Man, I cry out to God when I have a belly pain; I can't imagine going through all that suffering and still refusing to acknowledge Him.

The Sixth Bowl

Then the sixth angel poured out his bowl on the great river Euphrates, and its water was dried up, so that the way of the kings from the east might be prepared. And I saw three unclean spirits like frogs coming out of the mouth of the dragon, out of the mouth of the beast, and out of the mouth of the false prophet. For they are spirits of demons, performing signs, which go out to the kings of the earth and of the whole world, to gather them to the battle of that great day of God Almighty.
Revelation 16:12-14 NKJV

Now, God released three demons that will come out to gather all the kings of the Earth. They will deceive with signs and convince them to battle God Almighty in Armageddon.

And they gathered them together to the place called in Hebrew, Armageddon.
Revelation 16:16 NKJV

This battle of Armageddon has also frequently been taken out of context. This battle will be at the very end of the last 30 days. They gather not to attack Israel, like is commonly believed. The scriptures say very clearly that:

God released the demons so they could gather the nations to fight Him so they will be judged. (Please read Joel 3)

I will also gather all nations, And bring them down to the Valley of Jehoshaphat; And I will enter into judgment with them there On account of My people, My heritage Israel, Whom they have scattered among the nations; They have also divided up My land.
Joel 3:2 NKJV

They gather to fight Jesus not Israel

And I saw the beast, the kings of the earth, and their armies, gathered together to make war against Him who sat on the horse and against His army.
Revelation 19:19 NKJV

Note: Jesus hasn't come as a thief yet. Remember that when He comes as a thief it's not talking about Rapture but about judgement. It is at this point He says:

"Behold, I am coming as a thief. Blessed is he who watches, and keeps his garments, lest he walk naked and they see his shame."
Revelation 16:15 NKJV

The Seventh Bowl

Then the seventh angel poured out his bowl into the air, and a loud voice came out of the temple of heaven, from the throne, saying, "It is done!" And there were noises and thunderings and lightnings; and there was a great earthquake, such a mighty and great earthquake as had not occurred since men were on the earth. Now the great city was divided into three parts, and the cities of the nations fell. And great Babylon was remembered before God, to give her the cup of the wine of the fierceness of His wrath.
Revelation 16:17-19 NKJV

The Wrath of God is done! God will finish with Babylon in the last Trumpet. The greatest earthquake that will ever occur in all the history of the world will happen that day. We are not going to get into who the Mystery Babylon is. Even though it's a very interesting topic I think it's irrelevant for this book. You can read Revelation 17 and 18.

And great hail from heaven fell upon men, each hailstone about the weight of a talent. Men blasphemed God because of the plague of the hail, since that plague was exceedingly great.
Revelation 16:21 NKJV

One more time the people didn't repent but blasphemed God again. God is righteous and the judgment that He is bringing to the world is a righteous judgment.

Now in heaven there are a great multitude of saints celebrating and rejoicing in the Lord. Our time has come!

And I heard, as it were, the voice of a great multitude, as the sound of many waters and as the sound of mighty thunderings, saying, "Alleluia! For the Lord God Omnipotent reigns! Let us be glad and rejoice and give Him glory, for the marriage of the Lamb has come, and His wife has made herself ready." And to her it was granted to be arrayed in fine linen, clean and bright, for the fine linen is the righteous acts of the saints. Then he said to me, "Write: Blessed are those who are called to the marriage supper of the Lamb!' " And he said to me, "These are the true sayings of God."
Revelation 19:6-9 NKJV

N) The Second Coming

Now I saw heaven opened, and behold, a white horse. And He who sat on him was called Faithful and True, and in righteousness He judges and makes war.
Revelation 19:11 NKJV

Jesus will return to the Earth on a white horse, and we are coming back with Him. The time of His arrival will be at the end of the extra 30 days in the timeline. He is not coming peacefully, judgment is still happening.

Now out of His mouth goes a sharp sword, that with it He should strike the nations. And He Himself will rule them with a rod of iron. He Himself treads the winepress of the fierceness and wrath of Almighty God.

Revelation 19:15 NKJV

The battle of Armageddon will unfold and we, the Church, won't have to do anything at all. Jesus will take care of the armies of the world by His Word. This will be the Reaping of the Grapes of Wrath of Revelation 14.

And I saw the beast, the kings of the earth, and their armies, gathered together to make war against Him who sat on the horse and against His army. Then the beast was captured, and with him the false prophet who worked signs in his presence, by which he deceived those who received the mark of the beast and those who worshiped his image. These two were cast alive into the lake of fire burning with brimstone.
Revelation 19:19-20 NKJV

Like I said before, the battle of Armageddon is all nations against Jesus. Sounds like a great war and a big struggle for both sides, but it will be nothing like that. It will be like a 6'5" 220lb man with a flame thrower against an ant colony. The antichrist and the false prophet will be thrown alive to the lake of fire. They are the first to be cast to that place of torment but they are not the only ones.

Satan is bound

Then I saw an angel coming down from heaven, having the key to the bottomless pit and a great chain in his hand. He laid hold of the dragon, that serpent of old, who is the devil and Satan, and bound him for a thousand years; and he cast him into the bottomless pit, and shut him up, and set a seal on him, so that he should deceive the nations no more till the thousand years were finished. But after these things he must be released for a little while.
Revelation 20:1-3 NKJV

We believe that on the same day Jesus returned, the devil will be bound and chained for a thousand years. He won't be able to deceive the people of the world for that period of time.

The Millennium

And I saw thrones, and they sat on them, and judgment was committed to them.

Then I saw the souls of those who had been beheaded for their witness to Jesus and for the word of God, who had not worshiped the beast or his image, and had not received his mark on their foreheads or on their hands. And they lived and reigned with Christ for a thousand years.
Revelation 20:4 NKJV

The millennium reign won't start until the extra 45 days are complete and here is why. The devil will be bound for a thousand years and Jesus will remain for a thousand years too. But the devil's thousand years end before Jesus's thousand years.

Now when the thousand years have expired, Satan will be released from his prison and will go out to deceive the nations which are in the four corners of the earth, Gog and Magog, to gather them together to battle, whose number is as the sand of the sea. They went up on the breadth of the earth and surrounded the camp of the saints and the beloved city. And fire came down from God out of heaven and devoured them.
Revelation 20:7-9 NKJV

The only way that the time frame makes sense is that the devil is bound days before the millennium reign starts. So he is released days before the millennium reign ends. Satan will need a few days to deceive the people from all the nations to battle again against Jesus (stupid of them to listen to him, right?). Enough people to form an army whose number is like the sand of the sea, think they can battle against Jesus and win. It will take time to gather them. There are 45 days from the devil being bound, until the temple is cleansed, and in Daniel it says that the one who makes it to the 1335 days will be blessed. We have an extra 45 days here from His return; so we believe there will be 45 days between the devil being bound and the start of the millennium, and then 45 days between the devil being released and the end of the millennium.

Running Out of Time to Prepare

I believe this is the most important chapter of this book. It doesn't matter if the Rapture will be before, in the middle or at the end of the Tribulation, we must prepare for it. Many people believe that Christians should not prepare for the End Times. But they are very wrong. Before we talk about preparedness, let's first establish the reasons why we must prepare.

We will be persecuted during the End Times, hunger, pestilence and natural disasters will be great in those days. Preparing for those events will give you an advantage over the rest of the world. But the reason for preparing isn't to survive until the Rapture hidden in the woods, or in a secret bunker. The only reason that we want to stay alive in those days, is to lead people to Christ. Salvation must be what is in your mind when you prepare. I prefer to die early in the Tribulation preaching the Gospel, than survive three and a half years hiding somewhere and doing nothing.

I heard someone saying that it's ok to prepare for natural disasters but not for the End Times. Well, that doesn't make sense at all, because what will lead to the last seven years will be natural disasters. Great earthquakes, famines, and pestilence will be just the beginning.

Why did Jesus teach about the End Times and give us the book of Revelation? Why is the Bible full of prophecies and teachings about the Last Days? So we can prepare!

One of the main criticisms of Christians preparing for the End Times is that it shows a "lack of faith". But we have to believe in the Word of God and apply it to all that we live or do. Preparing isn't lack of faith, it's acting in faith. I'll give you some examples.

Joseph interpreted Pharaoh's dreams. Seven years of plenty followed by seven years of lack. Did Joseph lack faith when he suggested that they should prepare for the bad times during the good times? No. That was wisdom. If you know in advance that bad times are coming it would be foolish not to prepare.

A prudent man foresees evil and hides himself, But the simple pass on and are punished.
Proverbs 22:3 NKJV

Many people believe that God will provide for Christians during the end times. They think that He will give them food, and all that they need during the Tribulation, as He did with Elijah. As we already saw in previous chapters, there's no verse that says God will protect the Church from the Tribulation. The only ones protected on earth are the 144,000 and the Woman. Also, if we use that logic then we are in trouble, because among millions of people during Elijah's time of famine, he was the only one to receive provisions from God, and later the widow woman who helped him.

The reason for God to show you what is coming is for you to prepare. So if you believe it and act accordingly, that is faith.

Then one of them, named Agabus, stood up and showed by the Spirit that there

was going to be a great famine throughout all the world, which also happened in the days of Claudius Caesar. Then the disciples, each according to his ability, determined to send relief to the brethren dwelling in Judea.
Acts 11:28-29 NKJV

A real prophet stood up and prophesied a "great famine" throughout the whole world. What did the disciples do? According to the anti-preparedness people they were supposed to just believe that God would provide. But no. They were the people closest to Jesus in the history of the Church, and they knew more about faith than any of us today. They sent relief to the Church in Judea before the famine, that's preparing, and that is what I am asking you to do. But I'm not talking only about preparing food and supplies; you will need much more than that.

Train your people

One of the failures of the Church that was shown in the year 2020 was the lack of discipleship. We have made the Church so dependent on the pastor and the services. Many pastors were angry during the lockdowns because they could not have meetings in the Church building. They believe that the salvation of the believers depends on the pastor or the gathering together. It was frustrating for me to see that. "People need to be saved," they said.

People are not supposed to get saved at Church, they are supposed to go to Church after they are saved. Every Christian should be making disciples. But we are not making disciples out of our people and that must change now. If you are a pastor, or leader in the Church, and you haven't trained your people to do the same that you do, you are failing. Jesus didn't call us to fill buildings with people, but to make disciples!

Go therefore and make disciples of all the nations, baptizing them in the name of the Father and of the Son and of the Holy Spirit,
Matthew 28:19 NKJV

Jesus made disciples, and commanded them to make disciples, and those new disciples are commanded to make disciples. Not followers but disciples! That means that we all should do the same things that the Apostles did.

If you are a born again Christian you have the authority to lead people to Christ, and to baptize them. It doesn't matter if you have a leadership position in your Church, it doesn't matter how long you have been saved. No matter how unholy you feel, or how unprepared and unworthy you feel, you can and you should be leading people to Christ and baptizing them. You are also able to have communion in your house.

We are talking about the End Times, persecution will not allow us to meet in Church buildings. We all have to know how to make disciples. Preaching the gospel, leading people to Christ, and baptizing is for every believer. Also, we all as Christians have the authority to pray for healing, deliverance, and for any need. No more bringing prayer requests to Church from family members and neighbors. You pray for them on the spot when they ask you for prayer, and whenever you feel led to pray for them.

Then Philip went down to the city of Samaria and preached Christ to them. And the multitudes with one accord heeded the things spoken by Philip, hearing and seeing the miracles which he did. For unclean spirits, crying with a loud voice, came out of many who were possessed; and many who were paralyzed and lame were healed. And there was great joy in that city.
Acts 8:5-8 NKJV

Phillip went to Samaria by himself and the whole city came to Christ. It took one man to preach, heal, cast demons out and baptize a whole city. This one man wasn't an Apostle nor an elder or a pastor. He was just someone who served food to the people in need. He was a deacon. And in the times of the Apostles a deacon was not what we know of as a deacon today. His only duty was to serve food.

Phillip didn't act with power and authority because he was a "deacon", but because he was already acting in the power of the Holy Spirit, he was chosen to be a deacon.

Now in those days, when the number of the disciples was multiplying, there arose a complaint against the Hebrews by the Hellenists, because their widows were neglected in the daily distribution. Then the twelve summoned the multitude of the disciples and said, "It is not desirable that we should leave the word of God and serve tables. Therefore, brethren, seek out from among you seven men of good reputation, full of the Holy Spirit and wisdom, whom we may appoint over this business;
Acts 6:1-3 NKJV

Phillip and Stephen did great things for the Lord but they were "only" food pantry workers. That is to show you that we ALL must act in the power, wisdom and authority of the Holy Spirit. It is not the pastor's job to lead people to Christ, it is every Christian's job to lead people to Christ and to baptize them. The first thing we need to do to prepare is to train our people, and make them disciples who are capable of reproducing on their own. Remember that the purpose of preparing is to save people for Christ.

Create home/cell groups

This is something that all Churches should be doing all the time. Breaking the congregation into small home groups will make the Church stronger. But in times of persecution we will have to meet in homes like the early Church did.

If you are a pastor, start developing people to lead these home groups. If you are not a pastor or leader ask your local Church leadership, if they don't want to do it then you must do it on your own.

This group doesn't have to be of the same Church or denomination. It can be people who you know from work, school or your own family. I visited a big Church in Miami and I was amazed with the fact that 70% of the new members or visitors came from home groups. They came to the Church already saved. That's a good example of discipleship.

I used to be part of a Church with a wonderful home groups

program. We met every Wednesday in one of the groups that were available. The leader of the group hosts the meeting in his house and other members participate in the meeting.

The Church should have a list of all groups available for the congregation. (During times of persecution all lists should be destroyed). It will be good to allow people to decide which group they join and do it by cycles. For example, home meetings can start in January to April. You can join a group and you have to stay in that group for the following months. The new cycle starts in September to December and you can join a new group or you can come back to the same one. In the summer months the Church can meet in the building to give breaks to the leaders of the home groups.

The home groups program of the local Church must be supervised by the leadership of the Church. This will assure that no false doctrines, sinful spirits or divisions will occur in those meetings. Again, if your local Church doesn't want to do home groups, you will have to start one.

It would be foolish to get caught during the persecution having meetings in the Church building. The early Church held meetings in their houses.

So continuing daily with one accord in the temple, and breaking bread from house to house, they ate their food with gladness and simplicity of heart,
Acts 2:46 NKJV

Don't let anyone deceive you, we don't need a Church building to have Church. All we need is two or three gathered in Jesus' name. It is good to have a big congregation and all of that, but the size of the Church or the building doesn't make it a Church.

I hope that after 2020 the body of Christ has learned that we need to disciple our people and not depend on the pastor. The biggest failure that a pastor can have, is a Church that depends on him to seek God. No one that is well trained in the Church should fall away from the faith simply from not being able to go to the Church building on Sunday.

Now, during the persecution we have to be careful who we let in. We need to have the gift of discernment to know who is for us and who isn't. But we will make mistakes. Never let feelings lead your decisions. Our own family can be the ones who will betray us and hand us to the ones who are persecuting us. We may have to take a chance with someone that may end up a false brother. We need wisdom, not human wisdom but a Gift from the Holy Spirit.

You will be betrayed even by parents and brothers, relatives and friends; and they will put some of you to death.
Luke 21:16 NKJV

Know how to pray for the sick, how to baptize, how to do a small preaching or a Bible study. That's how it is done in many countries where Christians are persecuted today. If you are not a preacher or a teacher it's ok, just open the Bible and read it. Talk about the scriptures that you read and what the text means and how to apply it to your life. You don't have to be preaching in the meeting. You can read the Bible, pray and worship. But we must have a place to meet as a Church and reach the lost.

How to be Saved

If you are reading this book after the Rapture and there are no Christians around to tell you how to be saved, this section is for you. If you want to present the Gospel to your friends and family so they don't get left behind, then you can use this information to help them clearly understand what they need to do to be saved.

The salvation that Jesus offers is completely free, it is not by works that we obtain it, it cannot be bought. Adam made all mankind fall due to his disobedience. He wanted to take what he could not have, and when he sinned he caused the whole earth to be cursed. Jesus, on the other hand, came and gave us freely what we could not have without Him, salvation and eternal life.

Jesus said to him, "I am the way, the truth, and the life. No one comes to the

Father except through Me.
John 14:6 NKJV

Salvation comes from the sacrifice Jesus made for our sins; there is no other way to be saved. There is no other option, no shortcut, only Jesus. We cannot pay for our own sins without going to hell, another sinful human cannot pay for our sins. Our choices are to pay for them ourselves or allow Jesus to do it for us. No other religion can save us, no matter how beautiful it may sound. There is no philosophy that leads us to the Father, only Jesus.

Christ is the only door to heaven and rejecting Him will leave you with the only other option: the door leading to hell. There are only two places where we can choose to spend our eternity. There is no third place where we can learn about and accept Jesus after we die. Purgatory is not a biblical teaching, it is something that a religion invented, and what it leads to is only deception. It makes us feel like there's hope for the ones who die rejecting Jesus, but don't place your confidence in this... do everything you can to help your loved ones while there's still time.

And as it is appointed for men to die once, but after this the judgment,
Hebrews 9:27 NKJV

We will all be in the presence of God the moment we die. The decision to follow Christ must be made when we are alive otherwise it will be too late.

knowing that a man is not justified by the works of the law but by faith in Jesus
Christ, even we have believed in Christ Jesus, that we might be justified by faith in
Christ and not by the works of the law; for by the works of the law no flesh shall
be justified.
Galatians 2:16 NKJV

No good deed gives us the right to be saved, no matter how much you give to the poor or serve others. It doesn't matter how many religious rituals you perform during the year (especially the ones that are not in the Bible). We can't earn salvation on our own merits; it is good to help others and give to the poor but that should be the result of God's love flowing through us, because we have already been saved, not something we do in order to earn salvation. Good works are the fruit of our conversion but they are never the reason we are saved.

All human beings were created in the image of God and we all have attributes similar to those of God, but since Adam fell we are born in sin and cannot pay for our own sins in our own strength.

Who must be saved?

for all have sinned and fall short of the glory of God,
Romans 3:23 NKJV

The Bible teaches us that everyone has sinned, that includes me and it includes you, "all" in the original Greek means "all", so don't think that you are not included, we all need to be saved by the Blood of the Lamb. No matter how good of a person you think you are, compared to God we are wicked. The only good man was the one who came to this earth and did not sin even once, Jesus.

They have all turned aside, They have together become corrupt; There is none who does good, No, not one.
Psalms 14:3 NKJV

Now, since we know that there is not one person that is "good", what will our final destination be? God rejects the sin that is in us. He will not bring people who are full of sin into His presence. He hates sin, but does not stop loving the sinner. This is something that we have to be clear about without taking it out of context, God loves the sinner but because of his sin He is obliged to reject him. With pain in His Spirit, He rejects the sinner. He's like a human father that has a twenty-year-old son on drugs, in trouble with the law, stealing his belongings, disrespecting his mother and influencing his younger siblings to follow his path... the human father is forced to take the sinning son out of the house, even though he loves him as himself, he has to make that decision for the good of the family. Sin hurts people. It hurts the sinner and the one sinned against. God will not allow that in heaven.

The place to which our heavenly Father sends the children of disobedience is hell. A dark place from which, once you arrive, you cannot leave. It is a place of eternal punishment and complete separation from God. Hell was not created for human beings but for the devil and the fallen angels. When man sinned against God, we made a choice, if we continue in disobedience we will also be dragged into that place.

And do not fear those who kill the body but cannot kill the soul. But rather fear Him who is able to destroy both soul and body in hell.
Matthew 10:28 NKJV

But our heavenly Father is patient with us. God loves us with such a great love that when He saw humanity walking toward hell, He decided to come Himself to save us.

who, being in the form of God, did not consider it robbery to be equal with God, but made Himself of no reputation, taking the form of a bondservant, and coming in the likeness of men. And being found in appearance as a man, He humbled Himself and became obedient to the point of death, even the death of the cross.
Philippians 2:6-8 NKJV

There is no greater love than that. He himself came to pay for our sins and crimes. That is the most glorious miracle that Jesus has ever done in all of history. Just as in the Old Testament they had to sacrifice a lamb and shed the blood on the altar, Jesus served as the spotless lamb that redeemed all mankind from their sins.

The next day John saw Jesus coming toward him, and said, "Behold! The Lamb of God who takes away the sin of the world!
John 1:29 NKJV

Believe

The first thing we have to do to receive salvation is to believe, if we do not believe in anything that the Bible says, that is, what Jesus did for us, we won't reach salvation. We have to believe that God is real, that the Word is completely real and accurate. If we don't believe in the God of salvation, how can we ask Him to save us?

 To believe is to put all of our trust in Jesus, recognizing that He is our Lord, our Savior and the owner of our life and will. It is not something that is only thought of with our carnal mind, but something that is felt from our heart, and manifests itself in all our senses.

 There is an action that follows believing, something that moves us to draw closer to Jesus and to live for Him without fear of rejection, persecution or criticism.

But without faith it is impossible to please Him, for he who comes to God must believe that He is, and that He is a rewarder of those who diligently seek Him.
Hebrews 11:6 NKJV

 You also have to believe in Jesus, in His works, His teachings and especially in His sacrifice. Believing in the Lord Jesus is the only way to be saved, so it is a decision that everyone has to make on their own. Just because your parents believed and lived their entire lives for the Lord does not make you saved. Children cannot be saved when they are small since they are innocent before God, and are not responsible for their works, until they reach a certain age and maturity of conscience.

He who believes and is baptized will be saved; but he who does not believe will be condemned.
Mark 16:16 NKJV

 These were the words of Jesus to the disciples, stop and meditate on what He said. What do you think? The decision to follow Christ cannot be based on the imposition of a family member or pressure from a Christian leader. Many times they focus on pressuring people, forcing people to say they believe in Jesus when their hearts are not ready.

 Many come to churches and are manipulated to say they believe, but within them there is no conviction of sin, nor are they convinced of the reality of the Word, much less do they believe in the deity of Jesus.

It reminds me of an encounter I had in a church parking lot when I was serving in security. A man came to church drunk and was causing trouble. The internal security brothers removed him from the church and a brother and I seized the opportunity to minister. He changed his attitude drastically and I offered him the plan of salvation, which he refused. But he did accept that we pray for him.

The brother who was with me manipulated him into saying the prayer of faith, which the man drunkenly repeated. Although the intention was good, that man did not believe in what he repeated, he was simply manipulated. He said a prayer but never repented and didn't believe. Like him there are many "Christians" who have not shown the fruits of repentance because they did not have a real conversion.

Every person who believes has to believe for himself. It is up to us Christians to present the gospel firmly and let the Holy Spirit do His work in their hearts.

Repentance

Once you believe in Jesus you have to repent of your sins. Not because I am telling you too, but because in your heart you recognize that you are a sinner, and that you need to be saved from sin. Something inside you will bring your sins to your memory with the purpose of bringing your heart to repentance, that something is the Holy Spirit.

Nevertheless I tell you the truth. It is to your advantage that I go away; for if I do not go away, the Helper will not come to you; but if I depart, I will send Him to you. And when He has come, He will convict the world of sin, and of righteousness, and of judgment:
John 16:7-8 NKJV

After you sincerely repent of all your sins, the ones that you remember and the ones which you do not remember, the Holy Spirit will no longer remind you of them in order to make you feel condemned. But in times when you are playing with temptation, He might remind you of where He lifted you from, so that you do not fall once again.

From that time Jesus began to preach and to say, "Repent, for the kingdom of heaven is at hand."
Matthew 4:17 NKJV

Once you repent, the Lord forgives you of all your sins, all of them, no matter how bad they seem. Jesus paid the price for all our sins and when we repent we bring Him the "bill" that we owe. Jesus takes it, He pays it, and we are no longer accountable for what He has already paid. Once forgiven, those sins will not be taken into account when you present yourself before the Lord.

Repent therefore and be converted, that your sins may be blotted out, so that times of refreshing may come from the presence of the Lord,
Acts 3:19 NKJV

Repentance has to be accompanied by fruit. We cannot say that we repent if we continue to do the same sinful things, there must be the will to change and a contempt for what we did before. If you don't feel bad about what you've done, but excuse your sins so they don't sound so bad, that's not repentance.

Therefore bear fruits worthy of repentance,
Matthew 3:8 NKJV

To repent is to turn away from the sin we committed, to go in the opposite direction. You have to be willing to put what you were doing behind you and live a life of obedience. It does not mean that you have to be perfect to be saved, but in your heart there is the desire to do what God commands us to do and not to do what He forbids us from doing.

Doing your best not to go back to our sins is what God seeks. It all starts in our heart and in our mind. You may not do what you did before but you shouldn't fantasize about those things in your mind.

That is, if you had problems with sexual immorality in your past, do not spend time thinking about what you did with desire or satisfaction. This may seem impossible to you now, but once you're saved, God will give you a new heart and new desires.

In Jeremiah 17:10 it says that God judges the heart and tests the thoughts. So repentance has to come from our heart. That is what God is looking for, a humble heart willing to follow Him.

Confess

that if you confess with your mouth the Lord Jesus and believe in your heart that God has raised Him from the dead, you will be saved.
Romans 10:9 NKJV

Along with believing, there is also speaking what we believe. We must take out what is in our heart and confess it to our heavenly Father and He will move in mercy and cleanse us from all evil. You need to tell God what is in your heart, sincerely.

I believed, therefore I spoke, "I am greatly afflicted."
Psalms 116:10 NKJV

Now, confessing alone will not accomplish anything, it has to come after believing and repenting with all your heart. It is when we express vocally what is inside of us. Although He already knows what is inside us, it is necessary that we are the ones who cry out for our salvation.

Confessing cannot be forced or manipulated, other people making you repeat the prayer of faith will do nothing if it's not from your heart. It has to be completely voluntary. If we trick a person into confessing, we are not walking in the truth and it will not do any good.

The problem is that if the person does not have the desire or the will to give his life to Jesus, it does not matter what that person confesses, it is not real because there is no conviction of sins, and therefore there is no repentance.

Water Baptism

Baptism is an important part of our duty as a Christian and it comes immediately after confessing Jesus, and it is a condition for salvation. It is not an option, but a command. It is so important that Jesus taught us by His own example.

Then Jesus came from Galilee to John at the Jordan to be baptized by him. And John tried to prevent Him, saying, "I need to be baptized by You, and are You coming to me?" But Jesus answered and said to him, "Permit it to be so now, for thus it is fitting for us to fulfill all righteousness." Then he allowed Him. Matthew 3:13-15 NKJV

Once you confess the prayer of faith you are ready to be baptized immediately, it is not necessary to take baptism classes (although in many churches they give them because they confuse baptism classes with discipleship classes or new believer classes). I do recommend a brief explanation of what baptism means and what it does for us spiritually.

Baptism is not "works", it is a process by which we are buried with Jesus when we are immersed in the water, and we are raised with Him when we come out of the water. This is a physical act that has a spiritual consequence.

Or do you not know that as many of us as were baptized into Christ Jesus were baptized into His death? Therefore we were buried with Him through baptism into death, that just as Christ was raised from the dead by the glory of the Father, even so we also should walk in newness of life. Romans 6:3-4 NKJV

Jesus Himself told us what we have to do to obtain salvation freely: *He who believes and is baptized will be saved; but he who does not believe will be condemned. Mark 16:16 NKJV*

The apostle Peter, the first time the disciples won souls for Christ, showed us what we have to do to be saved.

Then Peter said to them, "Repent, and let every one of you be baptized in the name of Jesus Christ for the remission of sins; and you shall receive the gift of the Holy Spirit.
Acts 2:38 NKJV

 Baptism in water is a fundamental piece in the process of being born again. Once we are born again, then the Holy Spirit dwells in us. Now if there is no opportunity to be baptized, remember that God is merciful. You have to be baptized according to the Bible, but if it is not possible trust in the mercy and grace of God. But if you can be baptized; you have to be baptized. There is not a verse in the Bible that says that you do not have to be baptized to be saved, but there are several that say that you must be.

Now as they went down the road, they came to some water. And the eunuch said, "See, here is water. What hinders me from being baptized?" Then Philip said, "If you believe with all your heart, you may." And he answered and said, "I believe that Jesus Christ is the Son of God." So he commanded the chariot to stand still. And both Philip and the eunuch went down into the water, and he baptized him.
Acts 8:36-38 NKJV

The prayer of faith

 The prayer of faith (or the sinner's prayer), is the prayer we confess in order to receive salvation. Before we repeat a prayer we first have to be certain that:

 We believe that Jesus is the Son of God

 We believe that Jesus died for our sins

 We believe that Jesus rose from the dead

 We've repented of all our sins and want to turn away from them

 We believe that Jesus is our Lord and Savior

If you really believe in that with all your heart, then you are ready to receive the Lord in your heart by confessing everything you believe. Remember that if you are not convinced with all your heart, what you confess will be worthless.

that if you confess with your mouth the Lord Jesus and believe in your heart that God has raised Him from the dead, you will be saved.
Romans 10:9 NKJV

There is no specific prayer in the Bible that we have to say to be saved but here is a guide on how to do it. It is preferable that you use your own words, but if you do not know what to say, confessing the following prayer out loud with faith will also be the gateway to the kingdom of God.

Heavenly Father, I stand before you with my humbled heart. I recognize that I am a sinner and I need you to save me. I believe that Jesus died for my sins and rose again so that I can live in Him eternally. I confess that Jesus is my Lord and my Savior. Take my life and change it. In the name of Jesus. Amen.

If you confessed that prayer in faith, I congratulate you on making the most important decision of your life. Now the next step is to be baptized in water and in the Holy Spirit. Find a Christian church that preaches sound doctrine. One that will help you grow spiritually. Start gathering together with other believers and be sure you are taking communion regularly (John 6:54). If you need any information, or guidance, or if you have any questions you can contact us and we will be happy to help you. Write us at: outofendtimes@gmail.com

If you waited too long and are in the middle of the Tribulation, trust the Lord and don't take the mark of the beast!

Food and supplies

This is very important. We must prepare for natural disasters and famine. Also hyperinflation is a real problem we will face.

And I heard a voice in the midst of the four living creatures saying, "A quart of wheat for a denarius, and three quarts of barley for a denarius; and do not harm the oil and the wine."
Revelation 6:6 NKJV

This verse is often translated as "one loaf of bread for a day's wage". That sounds like hyperinflation to me. So we must prepare for food shortages and high prices. Hopefully when you are reading this book there is still time to store food and supplies for your family, and to share with others if it's possible. In a hyperinflation situation you must treat your currency as a hot potato, spend it as soon as you get it. The value of your currency will drop dramatically by the hour.

Many people believe that we are very close to the End Times but they don't want to store food and supplies. Well, you'll either end up in the government food lines or being a load to someone else. Don't be that person. Be the one who can self-sustain, or even better someone who can be a supplier to the needy.

Think for a moment about your kids during the time of famine. Maybe they'll ask you "Mom and Dad, why is there no food? We're hungry". You'll tell them "because the Bible says that this will happen". They will ask you, "if you knew that this would happen because the Bible says it, why didn't you prepare for it"? Think for a moment about how you will answer that.

I remember when hurricane Maria hit the island of Puerto Rico. Five days later people on social media started to ask for help because they were hungry. I'm not talking about people that lost their homes. People in perfectly fine houses without food after just five days. Everyone knew that the hurricane was coming a week in advance, but many didn't prepare.

The time to store food and supplies is now! This isn't the time to think about it but the time to act.

Remember this rule, don't tell anyone that you don't trust that you are prepping. I would include people that are not close to you. You have to be compassionate but also wise. Every person that knows you are storing food will knock on your door when food isn't available. Yes, we need to help those in need the most we can, but our family's needs are always first.

I myself have a rule that I may or may not enforce, "if I tell you to prepare, I'm free to not have to feed you later". The best we can do for people is to warn them of what's about to happen. I always share End Times Bible verses so they can see for themselves what God will do. It would be ideal to team up with the people in your home group. Everyone can store food and supplies to the best of their abilities, and share with one another.

Buy enough to supply for your family for a least a year. Rotate and replace products that you use. Canned food with a long expiration date is a must. Try the most you can to buy food that your family eats often. When you have enough for your family, then you can add extra food to share. Like rice and pasta. Please don't go now and get 10 shopping carts full in the supermarket. Don't draw everyone's attention. If you want to buy it all at once, do it in separate stores and on separate days.

Get hygiene supplies for your family for a year. Also it is recommended to find alternatives to toilet paper and feminine hygiene supplies. Think about the 1800's and how they did it. You can use portable bidet bottles to reduce the need for toilet paper. There are many prepper channels in social media that you can watch to get ideas of what to buy. Look at everything you use in a month and multiply it by 12. That will be what you need to store. I'll give you a list of ideas and must have items.

List of Supplies You Will Likely Need in the End Times

Bibles

Preaching and teaching CD (or even on tape)

Books on paper (like this one)

Long term food (if available)

Short term food

Hygiene products

Comfort food & candies (To keep morale & a feeling of normalcy)

Water and/or a way to get it and purify it

Ways to heat your house without electricity (if needed)

Batteries

Solar charger

Power generator

Light (Flashlights, candles, lanterns etc.)

Medical supplies (Vitamins, prescription drugs, First Aid kit, alcohol etc.)

Masks

Seeds for a garden (Learn how to garden now)

Canning supplies (Learn how to do canning)

Hunting supplies (cross bow/firearm)

Ability to make an outhouse or alternate way to dispose of waste

Get Right with God

Even if you think that you are already right with God please take a moment to read this section and examine yourself. What you have been taught may or may not be true. We have allowed many false doctrines, and lies from the devil, to infiltrate and dominate what is preached on our pulpits. You may have been lied to about the true Gospel and in the end it's your personal responsibility to study the Bible and to seek God for yourself. God gave us the Holy Spirit and promised that He would "guide us into all truth". You're the one who decides what to believe, and later you can't blame the preacher if you believed false doctrines because you didn't pray and study the Word for yourself.

I remember in an End Times movie from the 80's, a pastor of a church was left behind, along with a young girl who was never a true believer. She was blaming the pastor for preaching a watered down Gospel, instead of the true Gospel. The pastor answered her correctly; "you have the Bible with you." "Yes," said the pastor, "I'm guilty of preaching a watered down Gospel but you have the responsibility to search the scriptures for yourself."

You are responsible for reading the Word of God for yourself. If you don't know how, ask someone who does. Time is running out and we have many "Christians" in name only, people who call themselves Christians, but who are not living it! Where is your fruit? What are you doing for the Lord? Maybe you don't see it yourself so let me help you. If you don't have the desire to pray and to read the Bible there is something wrong! If all you do is sit in front of a TV watching everything except Christian programs, there is something wrong! If on top of that you never have a conversation about God, and you don't even want to go to Church, there is a lot wrong with your relationship with God! You don't do these things to become saved, but you will be known by your fruit and if you are saved, if you love the Lord, why isn't He even a part of your daily life? He should be your whole life!

Christianity is not a lifetime membership to a club that you signed up for once, and then you're in, no matter what you do, or how you live your life. Listen, it is not how you start the race, it is not what you did 40 years ago, it's how you finish the race!

I have fought the good fight, I have finished the race, I have kept the faith.
II Timothy 4:7 NKJV

You must fight the good fight of faith to finish the race! We are missing the instructions that Jesus gave us about how to live, and what to do for Him, because we don't love the Word of God and are too lazy to read it! If you think that you are good with God because you don't do bad to people you are wrong! You must live like Jesus wants you to live to be good with God.

God wants you to live in holiness:

Therefore gird up the loins of your mind, be sober, and rest your hope fully upon the grace that is to be brought to you at the revelation of Jesus Christ; as obedient children, not conforming yourselves to the former lusts, as in your ignorance; but as He who called you is holy, you also be holy in all your conduct, because it is written, "Be holy, for I am holy." And if you call on the Father, who without partiality judges according to each one's work, conduct yourselves throughout the time of your stay here in fear; knowing that you were not redeemed with corruptible things, like silver or gold, from your aimless conduct received by tradition from your fathers, but with the precious blood of Christ, as of a lamb without blemish and without spot.
1 Peter 1:13-19 NKJV

Reread that verse. This isn't an imputed righteousness. This isn't living in sin while God looks at Jesus and ignores your sins. It says be Holy in all your CONDUCT (what you do, what you think, what you feel, even your deepest desires). It says to conduct yourself in FEAR because you were redeemed with the precious blood of Christ. If you have been taught that you can seek sin, and then as an afterthought you say sorry, you've been led astray. As a Christian you are not permitted to "willfully sin". You have been made free from the power of sin. If you are tempted you cry out to God for help and you will be given the power to overcome that temptation.

Therefore let him who thinks he stands take heed lest he fall. No temptation has overtaken you except such as is common to man; but God is faithful, who will not allow you to be tempted beyond what you are able, but with the temptation will also make the way of escape, that you may be able to bear it.
1 Corinthians 10:12-13 NKJV

Repent! You must get rid of your sins and you must do it now! Stop believing that you are a sinner and that you can't stop sinning. (I'm talking to born again Christians). Jesus died for the forgiveness of our sins and to free us from the bondage of sin.

Now to Him who is able to keep you from stumbling,
And to present you faultless
Before the presence of His glory with exceeding joy,
Jude 1:24 NKJV

He can keep us from stumbling but many in the Church love sin so they believe and teach the lies of the devil, enough of that! You will be left behind. Please take the time to examine this for yourself. Please. It breaks our hearts that many who think they are good with God could very well be left behind.

Whoever abides in Him does not sin. Whoever sins has neither seen Him nor known Him.
I John 3:6 NKJV

This is why you can't stop sinning, you are not abiding in Christ! If you justify your sin, then you have some form of religion in which you are your own god, and you do and believe whatever you want. Don't allow yourself to ignore this warning. The Bible is the Word of God and we don't decide what it says based on what we want it to say!

What are you doing? Nothing?

Blessed is that servant whom his master, when he comes, will find so doing. Assuredly, I say to you that he will make him ruler over all his goods. But if that evil servant says in his heart, 'My master is delaying his coming,' and begins to

*beat his fellow servants, and to eat and drink with the drunkards, the master of
that servant will come on a day when he is not looking for him and at an hour
that he is not aware of, and will cut him in two and appoint him his portion with
the hypocrites. There shall be weeping and gnashing of teeth.*
Matthew 24:46-51 NKJV

 What are you doing for the Lord? Many of you think that
Christianity is all about you. You will be good and you'll go to
heaven. Let me explain something to you. If you don't have fruit you
are not in Him. If you are not doing anything at all for the Lord you
need to examine yourself. God said that He prepared good works for
us to walk in. If you're not walking in these good works you may not
be saved. A branch produces fruit when it is in the Vine. If there is
no fruit, are you still in the Vine? It doesn't matter what fruit you had
years ago, what matters is what you are doing for Him today!

 Please, don't come to me with the false doctrine that says you don't
have to work to be saved. To be saved you don't have to do work.
You are saved by Grace through Faith but you have to believe,
repent, and be baptized in water, that's not work! If you are truly
saved you will show the fruit. *Faith without works is dead.* You MUST
show fruit to know that you are saved. If you have no desire to seek
God and serve Him then how can you say you love Him? How can
you say you have God dwelling in you? Do you actually believe? Here
are some verses to back this up. (There are many)

*But someone will say, "You have faith, and I have works." Show me your faith
without your works, and I will show you my faith by my works. You believe that
there is one God. You do well. Even the demons believe--and tremble! But do you
want to know, O foolish man, that faith without works is dead?*
James 2:18-20 NKJV

*"I am the vine, you are the branches. He who abides in Me, and I in him, bears
much fruit; for without Me you can do nothing.*
John 15:5 NKJV

Every tree that does not bear good fruit is cut down and thrown into the fire.
Matthew 7:19 NKJV

Let your light so shine before men, that they may see your good works and glorify your Father in heaven.
Matthew 5:16 NKJV

in all things showing yourself to be a pattern of good works; in doctrine showing integrity, reverence, incorruptibility,
Titus 2:7 NKJV

"Then the King will say to those on His right hand, 'Come, you blessed of My Father, inherit the kingdom prepared for you from the foundation of the world: 'for I was hungry and you gave Me food; I was thirsty and you gave Me drink; I was a stranger and you took Me in;
Matthew 25:34-35 NKJV

"And the King will answer and say to them, 'Assuredly, I say to you, inasmuch as you did it to one of the least of these My brethren, you did it to Me.' "Then He will also say to those on the left hand, 'Depart from Me, you cursed, into the everlasting fire prepared for the devil and his angels: 'for I was hungry and you gave Me no food; I was thirsty and you gave Me no drink;
Matthew 25:40-42 NKJV

Now, coming back to Matthew 24, the good servant is the one who is WORKING while the Master is gone! What are you doing for the Master? The bad servant is the one who, while the Master is gone is doing NOTHING! Which one are you? Ask yourself what are you doing for the Lord? Are you teaching, preaching, evangelizing, and talking to your children and grandchildren about Jesus? Are you helping in your church (if you even go to one)? If you are not doing something for God, Jesus said that you will be appointed with the hypocrites.

Wake up Church! What are you doing for the Lord? I'm not talking only about the End Times but about everyday life. This is life or death! And you wonder why nothing is going well in your life, why your family is not saved, why people in your church are so carnal. I'll tell you why, there's no holiness and we are not doing anything for the Lord. Repent! Return to your first love! Run into the Lords open arms and ask Him how you can be pleasing to Him! Do it now! WE ARE RUNNING OUT OF TIME!

Bulk Order discount for all titles available at our website:
https://outofendtimes.com/store

Other Books by the Author

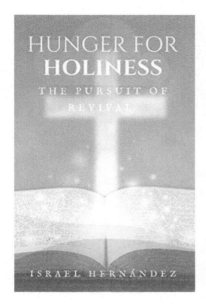
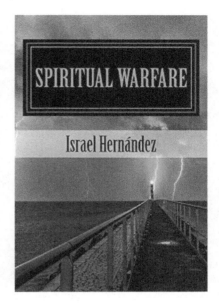

Made in United States
North Haven, CT
29 August 2024

56690221R00068